PUSHING DOORS
MARKED 'PULL'

Barry Gibbons was born in the first month of the first full year of peace after the Second World War – making him a definitive Baby Boomer. He worked for Shell, and UK brewing giant Whitbread before being headhunted to run GrandMet's UK food and drink retail operations. In 1989 GrandMet acquired the Pillsbury Group and Gibbons was posted to Florida as Chairman and CEO of Burger King Corporation, a classic sleeping giant. He and his team woke it up and Gibbons was hailed by *Fortune* magazine as a 'Turnaround Champion'. In 1994, still two years short of his fiftieth birthday, he decided to leave corporate life. Since then he has written six books on business, one on public speaking and one novel, and given more than 250 speeches to organisations around the world. In 2010, having returned to the UK to live, he was diagnosed with colon cancer. After surgery and chemotherapy he is currently clear of cancer and cautiously optimistic. He lives with his wife, Judy, in Bedfordshire. Their two grown up sons live well within mutual mickey-taking range.

PUSHING
DOORS MARKED
'PULL'

An unlikely life in three parts

BARRY GIBBONS

Rebel without a clue / Lord of the files / Cancer, my arse

First published in 2013 by
Infinite Ideas Limited
36 St Giles
Oxford
OX1 3LD
United Kingdom
www.infideas.com

A CIP catalogue record for this book is available from the British Library

ISBN 978–1–906821–81–4

Brand and product names are trademarks or registered trademarks of their respective owners.

Cover designed by GRID
Printed in Britain by 4edge Limited, Hockley, Essex

To Judy: TFT

Contents

Book Two: Lord of the files

Book Three: Cancer, my arse

Introduction

Who at my age really thinks about himself? We have fewer and fewer moments in which to reflect on what we have.

Tiziano Terzani, *A Fortune Teller Told Me* (1998)

It was not until I left home that I fell in love with my father. We were never real enemies before that, but we enjoyed an industrial-strength generation gap in a house that just wasn't big enough to contain it. Frankly, I doubt the Albert Hall would have made a fist of it.

He had been an officer in the British Army, stationed in India in the pre-war days of the Raj. Being born in the first month of the first full year of peace after World War Two, I was a definitive 'Boomer'. As I hit my teenage years, those two facts alone would have provided a basis for a generational disconnect, but other factors added fuel to the smouldering embers. There were factors in his post-war life that made him more conservative, and there were factors in my early life that made me more of a prick than was really needed.

I left home at nineteen, moving thirty-five miles away. By today's standards, a half-hour drive, but in those days it was distance enough to do the job. Mutual respect arrived, and then the mutual affection that had been hiding somewhere made an appearance. He eventually died, at the age of eighty-nine, in 1994, and I still miss him terribly nearly two decades later. I smile at the thought of him up there, chatting enthusiastically with a bemused Elvis.

I was thinking about him, and his life, one day – and a weird thought occurred to me. If you made a continuous chronological movie of his

1

life and then selected a few still-picture scenes – some of them decades apart – you would find it hard to believe that one man, occupying one body, for one life, on one planet, could play a part in such wildly differing experiences. Scene One: a wee boy in Limerick, Ireland, son of a British Army officer, prior to the Easter Rising. Scene Two: himself a full-blown British Army officer in pre-war India, complete (my favourite picture) with his own polo pony. Scene Three: the horrors of being a Japanese prisoner of war, experiencing the deep joys of daily life on the Burma railroad. Scene Four: A local government officer in the fading, post-satanic, post-war industrial north of England – a place where, should God ever choose to give Earth an enema, he would be likely to insert the tube.

Somehow he joined these unlikely dots together in a wonderful life. His family loved him, and – to my knowledge – he didn't have an enemy. And it was while I was smiling and basking in these reflections one day that it occurred to me that we had something in common, something more than just our DNA.

The link is not obvious. Whether by nature or nurture, we were like chalk and cheese in almost everything we did and thought. The list of differences would take up many pages of a book in its own right. His idea of dressing down would be to wear a cravat; my wife believes the word 'crumpled' was invented to broadly cover the way I present myself to the world. He was patient and polite to anybody and everybody who entered his airspace; I am fiercely loyal to close friends and family – and on a good day that squad numbers a maximum of fifty. If you are not in that squad, I am not rude to you. It's actually worse than that – I struggle to remember you exist. I have a late-life ambition to forget one new person every month. At the start of each New Year I relish writing out a new address book, celebrating each old entry that doesn't make the cut.

And so on, and so on. We were different – in all but one aspect of our lives.

If you think, based on my short summary above, that my father's time on the planet covered a few staggeringly different experiences separated by years of getting from *there* to *there* to *there*, I think I can match him. And that's what this book is about.

In fact, it's three books. Each one covers a maximum of a handful of years in my life, and there are (roughly) two decades between Books One and Two, and then Books Two and Three. Book Three is still work in process, and if you ponder about my father's dot-joining, I am sure you will raise a Jeeves-like eyebrow with me in trying to figure out how the hell I got from *that* to *there* to *here.*

Book One: Rebel without a clue

It's the first years of the 1960s, my late teenage years in post-war Manchester. It is a genuine working class area, though my family and I are in it but not of it. For a range of reasons, only some of which are understandable, I decide to rebel against everything and everybody. I am wholly ill-equipped to do so. I have none of the resources of John Rambo (muscles, knives, guns, technique), none of the coolness of James Dean, and am devoid of Bob Dylan's musical and poetic abilities. My hero at the time is Albert Finney in his role in *Saturday Night and Sunday Morning*, except I don't even have his near-to-zero sense of responsibility. The sexual revolution leaves London and heads north, but unfortunately swerves and misses my part of Manchester. But there are many compensations. A world is opening up to us teenage Boomers as no world has opened up to any previous generation, and we are not going to miss out. Even if we don't have an instruction manual.

Book One introduces the W Gene. Its full technical name is the Wanker Gene. Although it has never been seen under a microscope, scientists know it exists someplace beyond the double helix in the (mostly male) human DNA. It triggers a strange behavioural pattern in those who possess it. When things are going well, when recent life has been a sequence of climbing small ladders, this demographic, for no apparent reason, does (or says) something which provides a snake to slide down. It turns out that the author has a large glob of a virulent form of the W Gene secreted in a hidden cranny just behind his spleen.

I am thrown out of school at eighteen, with some qualifications but no references, and begin to splash about in the shallow end of life. I look as though I am booking a long stay there until a stranger gives me a challenge, and a smashing lass appears on my radar. This book ends with the challenge(s) these two pose me.

Book Two: Lord of the files

More than two decades have passed. From the *that* at the end of Book One, the opening of the *there* in Book Two takes an almost immeasurable leap. I am a dinner guest of Her Majesty the Queen, aboard the

Royal Yacht Britannia. It is moored off a secure dock in Miami, Florida. I have not long been appointed Chairman and Chief Executive of a multi-billion-dollar global business, headquartered in the USA. I am also a Brit – a Limey indeed – in charge of an iconic American brand. This book skims the rooftops of the life of a corporate rock star. The corporate jet, the aircraft-hangar house, the limos, the PR bollocks, the sycophancy, the back-stabbing, the front-stabbing, the air miles, the international adventures, the ball-fumbling (and sometimes recovering) and, above all, the seemingly impenetrable big-business barriers put up in front of doing anything that seems to pass the basic test of rightness. That smashing lass is now a smashing wife, and we have a family. We are, of course, 'expats' – now living just south of the city of Miami, which has some parallels with landing on the moon.

It is said that you can take the lad out of Lancashire, but you cannot take Lancashire out of the lad – and that brings good news and bad news. The good news is that the Lancastrian approach to turning around a punch-drunk sleeping giant of a company seems to bear fruit. A possibility is explored: that the W Gene might be controlled, and even harnessed, with positive results. The bad news is that the Lancastrian dickhead, plainly evident in Book One, is not above making an appearance – usually with immaculate timing. This book ends with the author in 'pondering' mode again – a common state for square pegs in round holes.

Book Three: Cancer, my arse

As we arrive *here*, it's all but twenty years from the last words of Book Two. In the opening scene I am in bed. Not my own, but that belonging to the Intensive Care Unit of a hospital in England. Another big difference between me and my father should be logged here: I swear too much. Again, it could be nature, it could be nurture – but I do know that my presence in the dressing rooms of amateur football teams of consistent mediocrity over a period of about twenty-five years contributed significantly.

I honestly can't remember the exact details of how I felt as I came round from major invasive abdominal surgery. I do know it was foggy, and voices were distant. I had some recollection of feeling as though I'd been hit by a truck. My body felt dead, but I had some movement in my arms. I felt the need to look under my covering sheet, not really knowing why or what I was looking for. There was the trunk of a body that didn't seem to be mine, a mass of dressings and tubes – and something else. Some things came back to me. That's what I was looking for, and that's what was urgent even in my subconscious. It was a colostomy bag. And it was on the left hand side of my abdomen. On the right hand side of my abdomen was a hand-drawn diagram of where it would be had it been positioned on that side. This is where it would have been had it been a *temporary* colostomy – to be abandoned when my colon was rejoined and normal (crapping) service would be resumed. Its actual position on the left meant that this could not be done. To quote Marks and Spencer, I had a bag for life. That fact penetrated my dulled and fuzzy senses, and I swore. Man, did I swear. Given the circumstances, the location and the audience, I have to say it was magnificent. It must have lasted about five minutes – *without repetition.*

Ten days prior to that touching scene I had been diagnosed with colon cancer. We were, as a family, back in England, so I had a bunch of friends and family rooting for me to at least come through the surgery. After the operation, the long journey of recovery lay ahead, to be followed by the delights of chemotherapy – defined quite specifically to take you to the limit of what you could stand, and then just a tad beyond that.

In the days and weeks that followed, I started my dreaded pondering again. In fighting cancer, you have a lot of things going for you today. Sophisticated surgery, complex chemotherapy and radiation are the big guns. Early detection, your age and genetic make-up, general health, diet and lifestyle, and the degree of cancer-cell aggression, are all additional factors that can sway the odds your way (or against you). But I began to wonder if there was an X-factor that you could bring to your own party. In the words of Popeye, I yam what I yam – and I began auditing that, and looking back at my life, to see if there was anything in my personal make up – mental and/or physical – that we could whack on the scales to help tip the balance my way.

If you get this far in the books, you will have some idea of what joins the weird dots in my life. I clearly have some abilities, but equally clearly I can illustrate the common-sense levels of a Greggs' steak slice – often within the same half hour. Of the seven billion people on this planet, there are about fifty, unique to me, who can count on me if the shit hits their fan, and who I am pretty sure I can rely on to at least hold my coat while I climb into the ring for a scrap. Is there any way this cast and this stuff could be harvested and used in my battle?

That's what Book Three is about. There are schools of thought, normally proclaimed by skeletal people living high up in mountains with goats in the vicinity, living on stir-fries featuring locusts and spending hours every day meditating, who believe that all of the above provides all you need to beat life-threatening maladies. My emphatic stance in the debate on this subject is summarised in the word 'bollocks'. Surgeons and chemists are sometimes essential, and there is a wealth of additional help and counselling available – but I do believe there is an X-factor you can bring to the cause. An even more unlikely possibility is explored here: that the W Gene might prove to be an ally. The trouble is, you have to know yourself quite well to understand what you have in your locker that might work, and the other stuff that's in there that could send you sliding back down a snake.

As Tiziano Terzani notes in the quotation at the start of this introduction, few of us really conduct such a forensic analysis of ourselves on our journeys – or, as a little known (in fact anonymous and unheralded) Lancastrian poet once described it, stop to pick the fly shit out of the pepper of our lives.

I've done it three times: twice of my own accord, and once forced on me by some virulent, aggressive, malignant cells that made an unwelcome appearance in my fundamental orifice (arse). The three books cover them.

Barry Gibbons
Ampthill, Bedfordshire
2013

Book One

Rebel without a clue

Your sons and your daughters are beyond your command…

Bob Dylan, 'The Times They Are A-Changin''

1

And did those feet ...

On the third Monday in January of the first year of the 1960s, a big cold hall was warmed by the steamy breath and crowded presence of about 750 boys, a couple of dozen men and precisely two women. It was the gymnasium of Audenshaw Grammar School for boys. Audenshaw itself nestled a few miles east of Manchester in the (still) industrial north-west of England. The hall also doubled as a gathering location for morning assembly, with which it was now occupied. It also trebled as an occasional school theatre, and quadrupled a couple of times a year as an examination room.

The boys were standing in ranks, with the junior eleven-year-olds at the front, and the rest graded by age until they reached the sixteen-year-olds at the back. The adult teachers (which included the two women) and the 'senior' boys of seventeen and eighteen, were up on the balcony. On the stage, at the front, were the thirty or so members of the school choir, and the Headmaster, Mr. R. I. Porter. He had that beaky look which is evident throughout the species, along with the mandatory dignified (albeit thinning) swept-back grey hair. The latter description was based on only a few sightings as his head was normally crowned by a mortar board. His noticeably big failing was in the chin department, where his Creator had compensated for giving him too much dignity by short changing him in the 'chinal' area.

The ranks of boys were structured so that a passageway about five paces wide was left open along the side of the gym, down which the headmaster would stride to the stage at the start, and stride from it at the end of the proceedings. In my experience, in the 1960s, headmasters of boys' grammar schools didn't walk or amble, they always s-t-r-o-d-e. In that open passage, backs to the wall, stood two very isolated boys, in school uniform. One was skinny and maybe an inch or so above the average height for his fourteen years. The other was a little shorter than average height, but compensated for that with an already Falstaffian set of measurements wherever you put the tape.

Let us zoom in with an imaginary camera. Assembly is nearing its end. A mini Church of England service is drawing to a close. Two hymns, chosen, it would seem, for their propensity to produce lustily sung choruses, have been sung. A few prayers have been read out by Holy Joe (the school Divinity master, blessed with this inevitable nickname) and some poor seventeen-year-old school kid has survived the 'honour' of being picked to read the lesson.

This ritual occurred every morning of every school day. Nobody present, with the possible exception of Holy Joe, held out any hope that the outcome would be an enlightened flock, but it was seen as a key weapon (albeit an indirect one) in the Establishment's Moral War. This was largely against masturbation. The main attack, of course, came from the pseudo-scientific threat that such activity would eventually damage your eyesight. This possibility was treated by the boys with the contempt it deserved, although it is an interesting postscript that not one of the heroes of this tale can now read a restaurant menu unless it is in letters of the size a tabloid newspaper would use to announce that the Queen of England had Aids. Without having been there, it is difficult to imagine the weight and the effort school establishments put behind this offensive in the early sixties. There was no war against underage drinking; although it went on, it was not seen as a big moral deal. There was not yet, of course, a war against drugs. So this was the great Cause.

I am indebted to Jeremy Paxman in his spirited work on *The English* (Penguin, 1998) for digging up a quote that reflects the physical and moral dangers perceived by the educational establishment in this exhilarating pastime. A Doctor Acton, author of *Functions and Disorders of the Reproductive Organs* (published in 1857 and still in print in this century) paints a picture of a boy who has incurred 'the large expenditure of semen':

The frame is stunted and weak, the muscles underdeveloped, the eye is sunken and heavy, the complexion is sallow, pasty or covered with spots of acne, the hands are damp and cold, the skin moist. The boy shuns the society of others, creeps about alone, joins with repugnance in the amusements of his schoolfellows. He cannot look anyone in the face and becomes careless in dress and uncleanly in person. His intellect has become sluggish and enfeebled, and if his evil habits are persisted in, he may end up becoming a drivelling idiot or peevish valetudinarian.

Let that be a warning to you.

Full-frontal threats got nowhere, of course, so the flank attack on this sin of sins was a moral one. They would push the idea that God – Himself, indeed – didn't want you to 'touch' yourself. That was right up there with the Charge of the Light Brigade as one of the top two lost causes of history. The ongoing position of the vast majority of boys present in that assembly was that, if God didn't want you to touch yourself, he'd have put the thing He didn't want touched in that unreachable place in the middle of your back, the one you can't get quite get to in the shower. As God had (thoughtfully, in our minds) put it front centre, it was fair game. To thank our God for his thoughtfulness in this respect we invented wonderful variations. The Doncaster Left-Hander required dogged determination. The Marathon (ninety-nine, change hands) needed sheer brute strength. But the great favourite was the SEWDI. For this, you would lie on your side in bed, trapping your arm. After twenty minutes or so, your arm would go numb. Then, if you did it, if felt like Someone Else Was Doing It.

Back to the morning service. With all the God-stuff behind him, Porter began his final announcements: 'I am pleased to tell you all that the school sports results on Saturday were very creditable. At lacrosse, our under-sixteen team lost narrowly to Manchester Grammar, while our senior team achieved a victory against the senior team of the same school. Our rugby teams also travelled to the same school, and our under-fourteen and first teams recorded creditable victories against very strong opposition. Unfortunately our under-fifteen and second senior teams were beaten, but overall our teams continue to improve on last year. My congratulations to all who represented the school.'

The hall was as quiet as it could be with 750 boys bored shitless. Slightly misreading the interest of the silent majority present, Porter carried on. 'I am sure you will all join with me in the nationwide congratulations being offered to Eric Evans, once a head boy of this school, who has announced his retirement as captain of the English rugby team.'

Eric was our only famous old boy, and our headmaster tracked his progress through life in great detail at these assemblies. I believe he was under the impression that the link between our hero and the divine atmosphere he'd created in the gymnasium would be such that we would see the error of our vapid ways and reshape our own destinies accordingly. God, apparently, loves an optimist. Then, a last shuffle of his papers. 'Finally, Gibbons and Summersgill will be in Headmaster's Detention tonight.'

With that, he swept up his black gown, descended the stairs at the side of the stage, and began his striding. The two boys previously mentioned were about twenty-five paces away, in the corridor left for striding, and the gap closed fast. It had already been a difficult service for the two of them. Exposed as they were, their lack of a hymn book –both having been irretrievably lost on day two of the new school year – meant that they had to mouth words which they made up as the hymns thumped along. Fortunately no record exists of their contributions.

Just before Porter got within earshot, the skinny one, who was the author, contorted his mouth so he could whisper out of the side of it to his companion-in-distress, Peter Summersgill. 'Gill, listen, let's play a game. I spy with my little eye... er... something coming towards us and beginning with... er... c.'

Gill couldn't handle this. Already naturally reddish in complexion, he went deep burgundy and spluttered the splutter you get when trying to stop an unstoppable laugh from surfacing from any orifice.

By now Porter was level with him. 'Clearly, Summersgill, Headmaster's Detention is a source of amusement to you. I will see you in the detention room when school finishes at 3.40 this afternoon. Perhaps you will be kind enough to share the joke with all of us present at that time.'

His gaze switched to me. I gazed right back, just as I imagined Albert Finney would have done in *Saturday Night and Sunday Morning*. Nothing was said, but the silence spoke volumes. He knew I'd dropped my buddy in it, and he knew I knew he knew. The ebullient and squeaky American President, Theodore Roosevelt, once wrote to his sister-in-law warning her of his brother's growing madness. He prefaced his warning thus: 'I am choosing my words with scientific exactness'. Porter also knew, that if I were to describe him, off-campus, with the self-same scientific exactness, the words 'complete' and 'prick' would be in there somewhere.

'I will see you also at that time, Gibbons. Again.'

Off he strode, and 750 boys filed out after him. Most of them wondered how, in the name of the Christ they had just been worshipping, they had ended up at a school which was buried deep in one of England's strongest soccer cultures, but where they were expected to play only lacrosse or rugby in winter.

Porter was right in one part of his short communication with me – the 'again' bit. As the sixties dawned and I hit fourteen years of age, my relationship with the school, or – to be precise – a handful of its masters, entered a new phase. If you have seen the film *Rambo, First Blood,* you will remember the moment when the aggrieved Vietnam veteran not only decides he doesn't like the hick town that doesn't show him any respect, but that he will declare war on it. It is stretching it somewhat to draw the analogy of a puny, pale fourteen-year-old, with legs like pipe cleaners and devoid of any muscular definition whatsoever on his body, to that of Sylvester Stallone who played the muscled military machine, but we did have two things in common. Our determination was intense, and our cause was just.

Pete Summersgill becomes the first member of the cast to be introduced. We went back about three years together.

2

Backbeat

In the mid-fifties, after I qualified for grammar school, our family moved house. We went from a dying textile-mill town called Mossley to a dying textile-mill town called Ashton-Under-Lyne. It was a distance of about five miles. To this day, I have no idea what a Lyne is, and what we were doing under it. Both towns were about ten miles east of Manchester, in the foothills of the Pennines, the hilly backbone of England. The climate was such that if you could see the distant Pennines from the centre of Manchester, it was about to rain. If you couldn't, it was raining already.

Mossley, which I preferred, had three claims to fame. About a century before, it had, for thirty years, been home to the biggest textile mill on earth. That had long gone. It also claimed to have housed the first fish and chip shop in England, a claim that was hotly disputed but not without some foundation. It also boasted a quite legendary railway station master whose fame was uncontested. He made his name on a rare state visit to the area, when King George VI had been persuaded to travel 'Oop North', and encourage the working classes after the war. He needed to – the war had been over for years but food rationing still prevailed; the drudge of daily life seemed a long way from the glorious promise of VE night, and the proles were getting a bit pissed off. It was deemed that the presence of the King among the Great Unwashed would convince them that the overall script still made some sense.

So, George did his kinging for the day, and his party arrived at Mossley railway station to pick up the royal train for the journey back to his palace, a decent claret and general civilization. As the King and his party stood on the platform, the royal train – which had been waiting about half a mile away on the tracks – started to advance towards the station. On the platform, a red carpet had been placed. The idea was that the driver would pull up with the appropriate carriage door exactly aligned with the carpet. The Station Master (and even the smallest stations still had one of these) was, apparently, a nervous wreck on his big day. The King, as only kings can, nobly tried to put his subject at ease:

'I say. Wouldn't it be awfully funny if he didn't match the door up with the carpet?'

The Station Master looked at him incredulously. No, apparently, it wouldn't. 'Just let the bugger try, your Majesty. Just let the bugger try...'

On arriving in Ashton, my parents decided against taking the easy, obvious and logical decision to send me to the local soccer playing, mixed-sex grammar school in Ashton, and chose one which was in Audenshaw, a few miles away. It was for boys only, and rugby was the sport of record. It involved two daily bus rides each way.

At ten past eight each morning, I got on the Number Seven double-decker bus at the top of our road, and started the journey. About half a mile further on, a boy called Peter Summersgill got on, with the same destination in mind. After a couple of such trips, we started a friendship that still lingers today – more than half a century later.

The half mile between our bus stops took a couple of minutes, but it was a million miles in culture and family background. Our house was in a secluded avenue, and we owned it. Pete's house was rented from the local council and was already starting to show an alarming list from coal-mining subsidence. His father was bringing up the family alone, his mother having tragically taken her own life not long before. My father and mother were spiritually upper middle class, although they were financially lower middle class; Pete's family was solid working class. Neither of my parents had a Lancashire accent, but you could cut Pete's dad's accent with a knife.

My father had been a professional soldier in the Indian Army, had an honourable war as an officer and POW, and had reached the rank of major – which he continued to use in peacetime, as tradition allowed. Pete's dad had an ordinary job, with no title. Having no title made him pretty much like everybody else I came into contact with in my daily life. My father's post-war job as a local government officer saw him settled in this essentially working-class geography. This was largely the result of him understandably falling in love with, and marrying, a Lancashire woman. The latter have many wonderful qualities, but tend not to travel well. She, my mother, tragically died when I was three. He then repeated the formula and married another one, who became my stepmother and a shining light in both our lives. As I write this, she is cautiously approaching ninety, and is so still in mine. As a result of all this, I spent my days in among working-class kids, but – as I said earlier – I was among them but not of them. Every night I went home to our aspirational middle-class oasis.

My parents were a delight. They were both remarkable people, who had a dream like everybody else. Their dream was for a higher *class* of living, not a higher *standard* of living – and there was a huge difference. They would have been happy to be short on cash flow if we (the children) could have attended private school or if the house had been in a nicer locality. But there wasn't that kind of money available, so during the day I mixed with the kids from the area. It didn't take me long to shape my dream. I wanted to be like them.

I also qualified for grammar school a year early, at ten. My primary school teachers, friends and family all seemed very happy with this Herculean feat but, as triumphs go, it was soon to be classed in the Dunkirk league. Pete qualified at same time as everybody else – eleven. My peers were, therefore, ten per cent more mature and ten per cent bigger, as well as being from a different demographic. Add it all up and, from the start, I felt like everybody was staring at me. They weren't, of course, but then Rambo was a bit paranoid, n'est-ce pas? I was downwardly jealous of everything and everybody, with their working-class ways: their love of soccer and a night in the pub, a bet on the horses or dogs, their laxity in disciplining their kids (my peers) and the fact that they had loose purse strings. An anomaly of British social structure at the time was that the bluer the collar, the more cash that seemed to be available on a week-to-week basis. They were, and did, everything we weren't and didn't.

I responded to this set of circumstances in the only way a paranoid ten-year-old could. I decided I would command attention away from the house from the get-go. By my calculation, the world was currently one short in its population of dickheads. I set off on a mission to reach levels of dumbness that could resource several villages with their idiots.

I started at ten. My crimes were limited – insolence, insubordination, swearing, gross abuse of school uniform, loss of hymn book, disrupting classes, skipping lessons, (occasionally) skipping school, losing school caps, text books, pens, protractors and compasses, having willy-measuring contests at the back of the classroom and Grand Non-Submission of Completed Homework on time.

At this stage, and I know it's early in the proceedings, I need to introduce you to the concept of the Wanker Gene. The verb 'to wank' is a simple piece of slang descriptive of the activity noted in the previous chapter. But the noun 'wanker' is entirely different. It's a form of address usually (but not exclusively) used between males, and can have a range of meanings. In a situation of road rage, it is a highly derogatory form of address, usually mimed with a fairly obvious hand gesture from behind a windscreen, and pointed at some fellow traveller who has caused upset. On the other hand (sorry!) it can be a semi-affectionate form of greeting between two close mates – as in 'Hiya, me old wanker', sometimes accompanied by an embarrassed form of man-hug. The concept of the Wanker Gene is different again, and we need to delve into the strange mind of Donald Rumsfeld, the ex-Foreign Secretary of the USA under George W. Bush's presidency, to get a clearer idea. Rumsfeld famously talked of 'unknowns we know about, and unknowns we don't know about' – and the Wanker Gene (the W Gene) falls into the latter territory. We know it exists, and is part of some DNA structures, but have never spotted it, even under a microscope.

A select few people have it. It is part of the DNA that triggers the wrong behaviour at the wrong time in certain individuals. Imagine, as you sail through life, that your boat of life emerges from a period of troubled waters and storms into calm seas with a gentle following wind. Within a very select group of people, the W Gene suddenly makes an appearance, and the owner of the gene, for no apparent reason, suddenly *decides to drill a fucking hole in the boat*. My DNA contains the W Gene.

There was a gradual acceleration in the scale and frequency of my offence list, and by the winter of my fourteenth year, at the start of one of the most defining decades in history, I was back across Rambo's bridge, and ready to take anybody on. My trivial anarchy usually started on the first bus ride, and didn't finish until I walked into our house, always late, and always after another detention. Frequently I would try and have my evening meal standing up, as my backside would be suffering from some variety of physical abuse suffered during the day. Before you leap to any conclusions about boy's schools and homosexuality, it was nothing of the sort. I neither witnessed, nor heard about, any such practice at Audenshaw Grammar School all the time I was there, although hindsight tells me I may have been looking and listening to the wrong people in the wrong places. No, I'm talking about a good old-fashioned beating.

There were two categories of beatings. The Headmaster could cane you, and, in my case, he did. Frequently. The minimum dose was six strokes, the maximum ten, and it always had to be formally written up in a logbook that he kept in a drawer in his study. Once it was registered, you'd have to stand over by the window, with your hands on your knees. An unwritten rule was that you never cried out, even for the tenth stroke of a ten set. By that time, of course, the cane was landing on a surface that was already roughed up a bit, but the code couldn't be broken. But it did bloody hurt. By the evening, your arse looked like it was hosting a close race between six or ten large earthworms.

Much more informal, and much more frequent, was the beating of the same target area with the sole of a sports shoe. This – euphemistically called a slippering – could be administered by any teacher, or (for the first few years of my time at Audenshaw) a senior boy who had been made a prefect. Such beatings produced a different pattern, with a more consistent colouring of your rear cheeks. A good one could get your arse looking like a Turner sunset.

Such events were considered to be in the normal cut and thrust of battle, but even I was outraged on the occasions such a beating was administered by a fellow pupil, prefect status or not. I got this shock very early on in my days at the school, as a result of taking part in a Wednesday afternoon games period. We were playing rugby. Gill (aka Pete Summersgill) had been selected as a hooker for one side, and I faced him in the front row of the scrum for the opposition. Using the boys on either side of him as leverage, he swung forward and gave me an almighty kick on the shin for reasons which are still not clear. It was out before I could stop it: 'Damnbuggershit, Gill!'

This was my favourite swear word, and I let fly with it with much the same effect as the Three Tenors would have on tight auditoriums forty years later. Right at the exact moment the scrum cleared up and left me facing the prefect who was refereeing our game. I was very proud of this word, having picked it up from Timmy Ardern, my neighbour next-door-but-one, a kid of the same age who went to a private school and who was so much more creative in his swearing than I was. It did not impress the prefect, a certain I. G. Weston: 'Gibbons, you will report to me after the game in the Prefect's Room.'

This I did, thinking little of it – as the potential of a slippering from a guy who was, after all, one of us, was not on my radar screen. That changed quickly as I was told to bend over. I contemplated some form of industrial action, but was told the alternative was to be marched, right then, to the Headmaster, with a high risk of a caning. Following the obvious logic that a Turner Sunset in the hand is worth two Earthworm Races in the bush, I choked back my horror at the thought of being attacked by one of my own side, and went to my death meekly. Weston – 'Iggy' as he was known – proved to have a strong and supple arm.

THWACK!

'Jesus, Iggy!'

'WHAT did you say?'

'Nothing.'

'I thought you clearly blasphemed, Gibbons.'

'You must have misheard.'

T-H-W-A-C-K.

'J-E-S-U-S!'

'That time I clearly heard you. Bend over again.'

And so on...

Iggy left for college soon after I arrived, and returned to teach at the school before I left. He actually proved to be one of the better masters, and never had cause to Turner my backside again. Only one other prefect did, a pompous twat whose name I have written down in a small black book. Today, half a century later, I know *exactly* where he lives, and it is only a matter of time before my curse strikes him.

Not all beatings were so civilized. A few masters were barely able to control themselves, and one or two occasionally lost the plot completely. E. B. Darlington (known as 'Eb' - we were very uncreative at sourcing nicknames) taught art and woodwork. I think he also formed an early role model for Hannibal Lecter. Poor Gill really pissed him off one day, and he (Eb) proceeded to beat him (Gill) over the head with his woodwork project, which was some sort of Heath Robinson bookshelf. Gill's nose started to bleed, and he stood in front of Eb flicking the freely flowing blood away.

'Stop that, Summersgill.'

'Stop what?'

'Don't you mean stop what, SIR?'

'Yes, Sir. I mean stop what, Sir?'

'Stop flicking blood like that.'

'But what shall I do with it, Sir?'

CRUNK.

This is my attempt to portray the sound of a wooden bookshelf being crashed (again) against a head of dark curly hair. I fear I do not do it justice.

3

Groin strain

In truth, when I started this I had in mind one of those epic poems. You know the sort – about a thousand rhyming couplets, endless pages of the buggers. Heroic figures everywhere, most of them dead or dying; towering infernos of some description on every other page; incessant whining. It would have been the first, I think, on the subject of Manchester, and some of those who sailed in her, in the nineteen sixties. That's what I had in mind. I started with a bang. Within minutes, I had the first half of my first couplet: '*A lemon-pale moon shadowed my best blackhead.*'

Seventy-two days later I gave up trying to find something to rhyme with it. Another approach was needed.

I have it on good authority[1] that well before the start of the sixties, in fact well before my own genesis, the incendiary, alcoholic American siren Tallulah Bankhead had a steamy affair with Randolph Churchill. I am not party to the information as to whether this was during or after the latter's short but meteoric career, and I assume it was not before. Steamy it apparently was.

It happened in England, outside London. On returning to the capital, and to her haven at the Dorchester Hotel, the lady in question cut his Lordship dead. She would not see him, or take his calls. Finally, he sent

---

1 Story attributed to Art Buchwald, in his memoir *I'll always have Paris* (Fawcett Columbine 1996)

her two dozen roses, with an attached note, 'How could you treat me like this after what happened in Manchester?'

Tallulah wrote on the back: 'Randolph, it wasn't you, *it was Manchester.*'

The italics are mine. Those three words will serve instead of about five hundred of my stillborn rhyming couplets. They are all you need to know about the place 'ere I make my debut in the City of Forbidden Steaming Relationships at the beginning of the Glorious Sixties.

Of course, I didn't know that it was that glorious at the time. I just wanted that shirt.

Fading from the school hall, we fast-forward a year or so, and our new scene opens in a crowded locker room. Now then – for those of you who actually keep records of this kind of thing – there were no actual lockers present. It was a small, bare room, measuring about twelve feet square, with clothing hooks fixed to the wall at regular intervals. They were at eye level for most of us. The floor was a cold, unforgiving concrete. In the centre of the room were two wooden benches. Eleven puny white bodies, in various stages of undress, milled about. Hands rooted about in sports bags, in the deep recesses of which were the individual secrets on which teenage soccer players had already learned to depend. They had also learned, showing wisdom beyond their years, to keep them from public view. Strange jars and tubes of pungent ointment would be included in there, to be secretively rubbed on exposed parts of the body before the game. The theory was that even if you weren't very athletic, you would smell as though you were.

The diet of these teenagers, at the start of the 1960s, in this working-class haven in north-west England, was such that there wasn't a face that did not include a flowery pattern of acne.

The general hygiene (particularly of the wooden benches) in the locker rooms which were provided for teenage weekend soccer in the same geography was such that there wasn't an arse that did not include a flowery pattern of blackheads.

It was late enough into September to be chilly, even though a watery sunshine would await us when we eventually ran out onto God's green and pleasant – but really badly marked out and terribly uneven – land which was serving as a soccer pitch. I was nervous enough, without having a lack of Fahrenheit add to my rapidly growing potential to shiver in front of a bunch of kids that would surely never forget, or, more to the point, let me forget, such an occurrence. C'mon, Mr. Ellis, where is that fucking shirt. I had known the next-but-last word in the previous sentence for several weeks, which was not quite enough time to instil the confidence in me to use it audibly, but I was getting there. I could use it inaudibly to great effect. None of us present could have known that its full, audible, theatrical debut from my own innocent lips was but thirty minutes away…

'Gibby, 'ereyar…'

Mr. Ellis clutched what seemed like an orange and black rag in what seemed like an enormous paw, and threw it over to me. He was crouched over the team bag, but this diminished silhouette didn't hide the fact that he was a big man and Strong Like Bull (as Tonto might have said). His hair was cropped impossibly short on top, but the barber had risen to the challenge and managed to get it even shorter at the sides and back. His face glistened with the natural ruddiness that accompanies its owner's body regularly getting outside a gallon of ale and shouting at racing greyhounds – none of which should cloud the facts that he was hugely savvy and had a memory, particularly on anything to do with sport, which could have seen him half-way up the bill in a vaudeville show. He was, and remains, fifty years later, a hero of mine.

A thin shaft of sunlight, penetrated the high, tiny, burglar-proof locker-room window and lazered down onto his sweaty forehead. Maybe the sweat was from the effort of the low crouch, or from the autumn sun, or from the gentle throw of the shirt itself, or from all of the above, but it didn't interfere with his aim. It flew straight and true, and I caught it as though my life depended on it. I believe I believed it did.

The thin, well-worn, cotton shirt was patterned in vertical halves – orange on one side, black on the other. The sleeves were the opposite of the colour of the side they were attached to. When you wore it, you told the world that you were playing soccer for the Snipe, a celebrated local boys team that was famous throughout our all our fertile teenage minds. This September Saturday, at the ripe old age of fifteen years and eight months, I was making my debut. I had yearned for it. It meant so much to me, for a whole variety of reasons, the main one being I was a skinny underachiever – generally in everything and specifically at soccer.

For a couple of years I had quietly fostered hopes of being selected for the England Schoolboys soccer team. In truth, the odds were against me. For starters, my school played rugby, and I was crap at that. As for soccer, by my calculation there were about 650,000 boys eligible to play for the national schoolboys' side, and I think 625,000 were probably ahead of me in the rankings. Of those behind me – given the time, circumstances and geography – about 20,000 would have been recovering from childhood polio. Most of the rest would have had verrucas.

So, this was the big time for me, and I was determined to do well. From the moment I had known I was in the team, which information had been given to me about a week before the actual game, I had been dedicated to preparing myself physically for the big day. Clearly, sacrifices were needed. With steely determination, I had not masturbated once during the week, and greater love hath no man. Or, more to the point, greater love could not have been haddeth by no hormonally-exploding fifteen-year-old.

The other pre-match details are a blur. Once that shirt was on, I just couldn't wait to get out and reveal the new, improved, sperm-retentive athlete that was about to be launched on the world. Mr. Ellis informed me that I was to play left half, a position now defunct in modern soccer nomenclature and fairly ambitious for this set of circumstances as my left foot has the effectiveness and efficiency of a chocolate teapot. Pah. Nothing was going to stop me.

You will have noted that Mr. Ellis had a high-profile role with this team. You are wrong, but only in the matter of degree. His role was much more than high profile. During the week he had a job with the (nationalised) railways, which funded his love of beer, racing horses and dogs, family and soccer. In fairness they were not always in that order. For the Snipe he was manager, selection committee, doctor, coach, fixture coordinator, transport organizer, occasional back-up referee and refreshment provider. He was our perfect role model. He was also the father of our best player, Sam Ellis (junior). Our home ground was an extension of his back yard, thoughtfully stuck there by the local council.

It was clear to anybody who knew anything about soccer that Sam Junior wasn't long for this level of soccer. He already had legs like tree trunks (well, teenage tree trunks), and a level of skill that was already getting noted in wider (eventually professional) circles. For father and son the Snipe team was a celebration of a combination of an unbounded love of the game and a means to an end. That end being Sam Junior's journey to success as a pro.

To play a team game surrounded by players generally better than you is a mixed blessing. For sure, your game can move itself up a notch and sometimes this is all that happens and you get by. This can be cause for congratulations, and a Mona Lisa-type enigmatic smile in the showers after the game. On other occasions, however, the fact you are operating on different physical and physiological wavelengths creates circumstances that make you look a complete tosser.

Fifteen minutes into the game, all was going to plan. I'd made no big mistakes, held my positional discipline, made a couple of tackles and was beginning to feel as though I might – just might – belong in this company. Then the ball bounced into our goal mouth, and the situation suddenly looked very dangerous. Had it not happened so fast, I am sure we would have panicked sooner. Suddenly, the commanding figure of Sam Junior, our captain (I may not have mentioned this detail, but I do not think this will come as a surprise), strode with colossus-like authority over to deal with the threat. His back was to me, and he faced our own goal with two opposing forwards starting to crowd him. I heard him shout 'Yours, Gibby' but I knew not of what he spoke. He wasn't even facing me, and was in no position to pass the ball to me so I wasn't even sure I'd heard the words right, what with not being able to actually see his face. While I was pondering all this, he executed his announced plan, which was perfectly feasible in his eyes (and with his skill) and back-heeled the ball through the tiniest gap between the opposition forwards, straight to my feet. All this while still facing away from me.

The ball duly arrived at my feet. I say 'duly' but, in reality, it took about a second. This was plenty long enough for me to metamorphose from being a newly confident, increasingly mobile left-half into one of those marble statues that grace the upstairs of the Uffizi Museum in Florence. You know, the ones with the little willies. As the ball reached me, I attempted to control it as a precursor to doing something equally spectacular with it to get us completely out of danger. What actually happened was that it bounced off my shin to a spot about two paces away. For a moment it hovered there, about eighteen inches off the ground, with everybody seemingly frozen in confusion. Then one of their forwards exploded into action, and kicked it powerfully back towards our goal. Straight into my testicles.

Let me digress a moment about nostalgia and soccer balls. Many men of my age mourn the passing of the old, unsealed, leather soccer ball. To them, it was a thing of beauty which became another victim as we gradually moved the game to something that can be played by – stay calm, keep your cool – women. Those that so mourn can have no knowledge of the collateral damage that could be achieved by one of these objects of war. If we could have landed a platoon of old English centre-halves, complete with long shorts, centre-hair partings and armed only with wet leather footballs onto the Normandy beaches in 1944, the Germans would have surrendered without a shot.

Inside the leather casing of these balls was a rubber bladder, which was itself sealed when blown up and then, in turn, sealed inside the case by stitching. Within ten minutes of the start of every match, the ball developed one of two properties. It would become either heavy from soaking up moisture from the pitch or heavy and hard from said moisture freezing during the mid-season winter months. In our game, we had just achieved the ball equivalent of Exhibit (A) above, and the immediate aftermath of it making a cosmic deep impact on my genital terrain (which was followed my me slumping gracefully on to the grass, trying to clutch the whole affected area) was that I felt what can only be described as surreal pain. I'd known nothing like it before, nor have I since – well, certainly until the events of Book Three.

Mr. Ellis, switching instantaneously from coach to doctor, came to the rescue at full speed. His total first aid equipment consisted of half of a rubber bladder which had been retired from its life's work of providing the inside of one of these balls. This he would fill with cold water, which he invariably lost during his impressive sprint out to anybody injured. Inside this bladder was a sponge. That was it. There was nothing in his medical armoury to remotely suggest the possibility of a there-and-then penile transplant with any confidence at all. So he pulled my shorts down and swamped my pancaked testicles with the little bit of water and the lot of sponge that had survived his outward journey. As I lay there, uncaringly surrounded by twenty-one laughing faces, I shaped my theory that God is actually a woman. If he had been a man, there is no way he would have put the penis on the outside.

I have no idea how long this treatment went on. Eventually, I felt my shorts being pulled up and Mr. Ellis lifted me to my feet. Have you ever seen a wildebeest stand up for the first time? I'm talking about the very moment that its mother has licked the afterbirth off? Then you'll know what I'm describing. Gingerly, and I mean g-i-n-g-e-r-l-y, I prepared, mentally and physically, for my first steps. I was suddenly made aware, however, that Mr. Ellis had done an about-turn and was steaming back towards me. The players looked puzzled and the referee pointedly looked at his watch, but the Big Man was not to be deflected. He reached me and in one movement pulled my shorts down again. Muttering the word 'two' to himself, he pulled them back up, and then began the return journey for a second time.

Sam Junior wandered over. Says he, with a straight face, 'He forgot to count 'em, Gibby. When he's fixed 'em, he allus likes to count 'em.'

Says I, in response, with a less than straight face, 'F-U-C-K.'

Let the record show I said it loudly. But still not loud enough for the referee or Mr. Ellis to hear.

The rest of the game proceeded without incident. Local census records indicate it was a further two weeks before I contemplated any sexual activity which could be filed under the do-it-yourself category.

4

Oh, Manchester

Our celebrated soccer game was being played on fields just east of the city of Manchester, itself situated about thirty-five miles inland from the port of Liverpool. As a centre of population, Manchester boasted a long history going back to Roman times. It was originally named, it seems uniquely, after a tit (Mamucium). Whether this was in line with the legend that the first point of occupation was next to a breast-shaped hill, or whether it reflected, as I like to think, some visionary legionnaire staring into his equivalent of a spread of Tarot cards and seeing a crude but accurate single-word describing the stereotypical professional soccer player who represented the Manchester team I was to support some two thousand years later, can only be conjecture.

If the city's history stretched back to Roman times, its true heritage had been moulded during the last hundred and fifty years. It had been a palace of the Industrial Revolution, and its throne had seated King Cotton. For a period in the nineteenth century it was the most modern city on earth, reflecting at the same time the technical glory and social misery that came as a full package with such progress.

By the 1950s, the glory had all but gone. India held on to the markets for textiles we lost during the temporary deflection of World War Two, and a rebuilt Japan was stealing ahead technically. The horrendous social conditions of the unregulated and unenlightened capitalism of the previous century had eased, but this was still a solid working-class area. There was tension and bitterness at the declining and disappearing primary industries, and not much new stuff was coming in to replace it.

Organized labour, with a mission to defend the indefensible, was about to enter its golden era.

As the sea is to the occupants of a sea side town, soccer was ever present in this culture. Some (very few) made their living from it. Others played it as a hobby. There was an endless supply of Mr. Ellises, guys who had played enthusiastically as amateurs and now took over non-playing roles. If you weren't involved in it directly, you supported it – either one of the city's two professional teams, or another of the half dozen or so 'lesser' teams in the industrial hinterland. If you didn't do any of the above, you talked about it, endlessly, in the pub. There were only two rules to this cultural sub-dimension: first, you must, almost tribally, play for and/or support a team; second, you must always have an opinion.

Manchester's two professional teams had experienced success in the fifties, and almost everybody in the city supported either the Reds (United) or the Sky Blues (City). How you picked one or the other, or how it was picked for you, was unique to every individual, and only becomes boring when you have heard it, say, a hundred and fifty times – although if you are all drunk, it can run to a few more repetitions. Some say the Reds had a Catholic heritage, with the Sky Blues having more of a Protestant affinity. Others point out that the Sky Blues generally had a 'better class of person' in their crowd, whereas the Reds found their fertile ground at the raggedy-arsed end of the working class. For some it was easy; you followed your father's choice, a route supported by most mothers as the alternative did not always provide for a happy home on the Sundays after their two respective games.

I am quite clear what latched me on to the Sky Blues, setting me up for a lifetime's pursuit of underachievement and mediocrity. My dad had taken me to Maine Road, the rather tatty stadium home of Manchester City, a couple of times. On a few other occasions I'd been with my uncle Jack to Manchester United's gloomy ground at Old Trafford. Both teams would regularly attract crowds in excess of 50,000, albeit United more often than City. These people would crowd into stadiums that, if comfort and sanitation were to be included in the criteria for a successful afternoon's visit, should have held half that number. If you needed to go to the toilet to lay a cable at half time, it was not an experience of memorable sophistication. If you just needed a wee, such were the barriers put between you and a place of official relief that many didn't bother to leave their place in the grandstand. The big professional soccer clubs of the day had clearly studied Himmler's recently advocated theory of customer service.

As it happened, neither my dad nor my uncle influenced my fateful choice. It all came down to a much decorated German paratrooper.

Bernhard Carl Trautmann[2] had been captured by the American army in the later stages of the war. He was shipped back to the UK, and served as a POW near Liverpool. After the war, he stayed in England working in bomb disposal teams and playing local soccer. His prowess as a goalkeeper was noted and he joined Manchester City. He gave an early indication that he was learning the local way of life quickly by fathering a child with a local lass, and then marrying someone else. On his joining City, there were threats in the press and abusive letters galore but it was indicative of the club, and their paradoxical style of getting a few things really right amidst getting a lot of things really wrong, that they rose above all that and made him welcome. His spectacular play soon made him a national hero rather than a villain, albeit in his adopted England rather than his native Germany. He captured my schoolboy heart without qualification.

In the mid-fifties, City reached the cup final twice, winning the second one. During this game, Trautmann – now universally known as 'Bert' – broke a bone in his neck, but refused to go off. All my comic books of the time portrayed German soldiers as hard-helmeted moronic losers, but here was this guy, with glorious blond hair flying in the wind, dancing through pain and playing like a hero. You couldn't make this stuff up.

After the cup final triumph, City's fortunes faded. In my official complete history of the club, the decade of 1956–65 is entitled 'Losing Supremacy', which is somewhat flattering because you can only really lose what you had, and 'supremacy' is a little misleading. If the official history of, say, the island of Tenerife has a chapter about losing supremacy, then it is, indeed, a fair reflection of what we did. But it does need to be seen in that context.

Our decline made no difference to Bert. His heroism just took on another dimension. Year after year he stood as the only barrier between the team and relegation, single-handedly saving everything the opposition threw at him in the last few vital matches of the season. Deserved 4-0 defeats were converted into undeserved tied games, and the precious resultant points would keep adding up till we were safe. Until, of course, next year, when it was all repeated. It was the Alamo, and Bert was my Davy Crockett. Unfortunately, by the time he hung up his boots

2   Trautmann died in 2013 just as I was completing Book Three. RIP Bert.

to be replaced by an unimaginative English (relative) midget called Harry Dowd, it was beyond me to switch my allegiance to any other team. A life sentence had started.

It is conceivable that Bert was doing his thumb-in-the-dyke act on that very Saturday, at that very time, not ten miles away from where Mr. Ellis was coaxing my testicles from their temporary resting place just behind my pancreas. I like to think so. It did cross my mind that we shared something on that day. The pain of his broken neck and the pain of my flattened knackers were the price we heroes must pay for the cause.

I cannot remember the result of our game, but before we leave it completely, I must introduce you to two more members of the team. We've met Sam Junior, whose spectacular legs were matched *in extremis* up top by wondrous acne. He would eventually play professional soccer at the highest level, and he wasn't the only class act in the team. We had a languid inside forward called Kevin Randall who would also make a living at the sport, but our focus now needs to switch to our left-sided forwards. The inside left was Stuart Kirk, a small dapper kid, always coolly dressed, whose already slightly receding hairline gave him an appearance of maturity and sophistication that sat well with him – until he got himself outside about three pints of bitter ale. Then he came back to being one of us. After six pints he would pass us and leave us behind, with maturity and sophistication profoundly noticeable by their absence. His soccer reflected this Dr. Jekyll – neat, tidy and classy – assisted by a wonderful left foot, and he, too, would rapidly progress from this base to a higher (in his case semi-professional) standard.

On the wing of another local team was Geoff Barratt, somewhat skilled but enormously fast, though problems arose when he had to run in anything other than a straight line. It was like having Road Runner up front for us. He would move on to a prolonged and honourable career as a short distance sprinter, which he would complement and fund by operating an unlikely market stall for twenty-odd years. His specialty would be reject shirts, and, bearing in mind the characteristics of his market demographics, his particular niche would emerge as male working shirts, neck sizes seventeen to twenty-four inches. There are many who go through life without having bodies of that circumference.

By September 1961, we had another headmaster, the redoubtable Mr. K. D. Exeley who changed precisely nothing in the school's modus operandi. September also saw this cast of four (Ellis, Gibbons, Kirk and Barratt) soon to be bound by a force other than boys soccer...

Some thirty-five miles away, at around the same time, another four youngsters, John Lennon, Paul McCartney, George Harrison and Pete Best, were also getting together. I mention this only for those of you interested in this kind of spooky coincidental element.

5

High school confidential

To over-emphasize beatings as a reflection of the daily life of the school is to be guilty of two sins. It would omit the fact that school life had many dimensions that were both positive and enjoyable. It would also miss the point that it was no big deal in the culture of the time. You misbehaved, you got hit, you all moved on. It was a single tiny symptom, however, of a mid-century English societal disease that was much broader than the biggest classroom. Like someone who inhales other people's smoke, I suffered indirectly.

This book is not a treatise on the pratfalls of the British class system. But nowhere, and at no time, was its bone-headed vapidity more evident than in the 1950s English boys-only grammar school. The sickness does not centre on the lifestyles and attitudes of privileged few; most nations have an elite and Britain could, on balance, do a lot worse. The problem is the sickly aspiration of the majority of the rest of the nation to be like them, and here's where we are unique – it's not a money thing. As I found out from personal experience later, in the USA inequality is rampant – but it's strictly a wealth issue. In the UK, those aspiring to the elite often have more disposable money than their targets, but that's not what they want. They want to look like them and behave like them. It's an attitude that makes a successful shoe salesman turn up for a weekend social event with his peers (let's say watching his kids play soccer), wearing a waxed farm jacket that looks as though it has been dragged through a field of cow shit, green Wellingtons (preferably with buckles on) and a houndstooth flat cap. The Full Monty will be completed by him driving a four wheel drive S.U.V. The full impression will be that he has been dragged reluctantly away from farming his lower 40,000 acres, and has popped in on his way to the polo match.

Nowhere was this cow-shit-coated, wannabe culture more prevalent than in an English boys-only grammar school at a time when one of them played unwilling host to my visit. The privileged schooling in the UK was – and still is – is the private (fee-paying) system. Only one in fifteen families can afford it, but it still determines one in four university places. Over fifty per cent of Oxford and Cambridge university places are private school-sourced, thus guaranteeing the continuum of influence and power. The whole idea is an insult to the principles of a meritocracy or democracy, but you know what? That's just what the rest of the population actually want. Polls indicate that half the UK population would send their kids to private schools if they could afford to. The mid-century grammar schools, although meant to be something entirely different, were forced to reflect that frustration.

The post-war Education Act provided for three types of free education for eleven- to fifteen-year-olds: grammar schools, secondary schools and the technical schools. The grammar schools were designed for academic high flyers who would take up only about five per cent of the school population, with fifteen per cent pursuing specialized technical vocation training, and the secondary schools taking the core eighty per cent. It never happened. The perceived social cachet of the grammar school drove local authorities, under electoral pressure from parents, to widen the grammar school franchise to about twenty-five per cent of the pupil population, with only a tiny five per cent focusing on technology. The secondary modern schools ended up preparing working-class children for working-class jobs. The whole system was shaped by the two great common British characteristics – envy and malice.

Thus it was that schools like Audenshaw ended up simply aping a lot of the ways of private schools. The boys-only aspect was a bad start, but was indicative of many plagiarist's abilities to steal only the bad and miss the good. Instead of producing sixteen-year-old kids ready to go into wider society with balanced sensitivities toward the opposite sex, they produced paranoid wankers (the noun – i.e. the derogatory version) who thought girls were from another planet. Masters trailed about in black gowns. First years were called 'fags', and prefects could slipper fellow students. Pupils were divided into 'houses' to ape the *esprit de corps* of a boarding school campus. Beatings were a daily ritual. We played rugby as the school sport because that was what the upper-class schools did - this despite being in dark satanic mill-town, soccer-mad, Manchester. At lunchtime every day, every kid I knew gobbled his food down and raced outside to play soccer on the field – but the school still didn't take the hint.

The curriculum suffered in the same way. The best teachers, of course, ended up in the private schools, so the public system got second best. Many of these guys (in our case all but two were male) were losers, and taught like it. Whatever skills and interest they once possessed had atrophied. Year after year they would turn out the same old tired and tedious claptrap, devoid of any modern or even original thinking. Anthony Crosland, a senior post-war Labour Party politician who fancied himself a place in history as one of the seminal socialist intellectuals of the age but who would eventually be remembered only for having a disarmingly pretty wife, did have one sound idea. His personal declared goal was '…to destroy every fucking grammar school in the country'. Had he stayed around, I might have broken one on of my future life rules and voted.

In these schools, of course, Latin was a compulsory subject until you were sixteen. Useful modern languages, by contrast, were electives. Telecommunications, the automobile, internationalism and oodles of new technology exploded all around us, but at sixteen we were hopelessly ill-equipped to understand them and live in that world. When I eventually left school, I had a backside like suede leather, could play rugby (badly), was terrified of anything with tits and could conjugate three Latin verbs if I was given a week's notice. All very handy. Unfortunately the British Empire had all but gone, so these talents – which would have given me a perfect profile for a civil service posting in pre-war Madras – were not in high demand.

My early fiery academic comet also fell abruptly from the sky. I entered Audenshaw as a bright kid, an academic year ahead of my peers. By the time I reached fifteen, however, it was clear that Rambo Lite was spending much of his waking time pissing on his own slippers. My W Gene was wiping off its afterbirth, and beginning to kick in. I lost all that early impetus. I would have to give up the year's 'advantage' and stay down. It seems my dedication to time-consuming causes such as removing the rubber peak from inside the cloth of my school cap (so that it could bend and wave in line with my Gene Vincent hair style), caused my pursuit of intellectual excellence to drop off.

At sixteen, you were faced with your external and national GCE examinations, which would equip you for life outside school, or provide a passport to a university-entrance-focused two years in the sixth form. You took multiple subjects, often mixing arts and sciences, and it was a numbers game. Anywhere between five and eight signalled that the whole circus had been worthwhile, although it was possible to get more and many got less. How many you entered was determined by your school, and usually the result of a 'mock' set of exams taken early in your sixteenth year. I took mine in good heart. For the Physics exam, my desk placing in the school hall was on the stage at the front of the hall, neatly situated right next to the lighting console. After writing my name, and rapidly coming to the conclusion that there must have been some mistake and that I had wondered into the advanced Arabic exam, I entertained myself for three hours by *ever so slowly* dipping and then raising the lighting levels throughout the hall. My delight in getting away with it (and watching 120 heads slowly lower to get nearer the paper as it darkened, and rise with some mystic synchronicity as the lighting level went up again), was mitigated on my exit only by the revelation that it had been the correct exam for me after all.

Mr. Exeley broke the news, which really was unusual. Such a summons usually meant but one thing for me, and I presumed I was up for an earthworm job. I was naturally delighted to be informed that I was not to be caned, but as I had failed the mock exams to a quite unprecedented degree, he had chosen to personally break the news to me that Audenshaw would 'not be wasting any taxpayer's money' by entering me for the external GCEs. In addition he informed me that I would stay down and repeat my fifth year. My *combined* total in Physics *and* Chemistry turned out to be seven per cent – out of a possible two hundred per cent. Chemistry just stole ahead with an eye-popping four per cent, so he took another decision for the good of me and the school. Whatever life had in store for me, British science was to be protected by my future absence from anything to do with it. It was a welcomed divorce, I suspect by both parties, and there have been no signs of reconciliation in the half-century since. I had gone into his study expecting a caning, and came out my arse untouched, and armed with the brilliant news that I was to stay down, join my own age group, and that I would never do science again. Some days are diamonds.

They let me take Art GCE in my fifteenth year, on the grounds that I was too good at it to fail, so I chalked up one GCE that summer. For some reason, if you put a Bunsen burner in my hand, disaster often struck – but if you put a charcoal pencil in there, something good emerged. It is/ was a talent that didn't do me much good then, and hasn't since. Waste.

My parents were nonplussed about the tsunami of negative news, trying to figure out where a wheel had fallen off when they had done everything according to their operations manual. As I waited for my Art result, the news broke in July that my beloved Manchester City had sold Denis Law to an Italian soccer club. We had signed him as a twenty-year-old about fifteen months previously, being brave enough to pay a British transfer record for him. That showed vision. It was clear from the get-go that this was *the* player of his generation, the kind you could build a dynastic team around. So we sold him for a quick profit. The vision had faded into blind greed. The outlook for my beloved team matched that of my immediate academic future: heavy clouds were gathering.

Gill passed a few GCEs and left school to make his way in the (still) dark-ish, satanic-ish outside world, and it was to be some years before we linked up again. The class of the year behind me, which I was now to join, was full of bright young things. Quite a few of them seemed to be able to have fun, be good at sports and still pass exams. Sam Ellis, Stuart Kirk and Geoff Barratt were among them. All they needed was a village idiot.

6

Summertime blues

'Where's Sam?'

'O'er by t' bags, paddin' up.'

I made my way round the back of the main school building, continuing my search for Ellis. It was April 1962, with the inaugural Snipe soccer game a few months behind us. We were just back at school from the Easter vacation, a time of year when Manchester's weather plays some of its dirtiest tricks. Just when you think the slush, sleet, snow, cold and drizzle is over for a year, it can still spring a nasty late freeze on you. But not today. The day had all the promise of summer soon ahead, and fittingly we were engaged in the first inter-house cricket match of the year.

Bert Trautmann had just completed his annual task of keeping Manchester City in the First Division, and across the land soccer goalposts were coming down to go into store for the summer. In their place, cricket squares – those precious areas of turf that had been protected for six months by an assortment of rickety fences – were being mowed and prepared by mysterious men known as 'groundsmen'. These guys were always old, ruddy faced and talked about nothing other than strange things like loams. Or so it seemed to me. They also had something else in common. I have met about fifty groundsmen during the course of my life, and between them they have totalled about eight teeth.

I found Sam. The 'bags' referred to were the big canvas holdalls that contained the armour associated with the vicious game of inter-house school cricket. One such bag would be allocated to each team, and it would contain an inventory of protective leg pads, batting gloves, bats, wickets, hard leather cricket balls and invariably two, and only two, 'boxes'. These were the protective cups you shoved down the front of your underpants when you went into bat to cater for the likelihood of you swinging your bat at a ball, missing it by a good six inches, and then having your undefended penis and/or testicles provide the only impediment to a hard cricket ball heading off on a journey of a couple of hundred yards at speed. Some forty years later as I shower every day and floss my teeth, I often wonder at how we all survived what must have been the substantive heath risk involved in eleven teenagers walking off the pitch after being given out and immediately thrusting one hand down the front of their pants to retrieve, not unlike a magician in early training, a warm plastic cup-like object, glistening with groinal sweat and Christ knows what other secretions, which would then be handed to the next kid, who would reverse this process without a second thought. By the end of a long summer's day, the inside of one of those must have made the immediate environs of Chernobyl seem like a butterfly meadow in Provence.

I said that I found Sam. I did, but that simple statement does not do it justice. We must rewind the tape otherwise you will not get the full impact. We discovered in a previous chapter that he was a strapping lad, already north of six feet tall and blessed with the very solid legs of someone who knows that he will play soccer for a living one day. As we proceed in a northerly direction up the torso, we find a mop of bright red hair – and I mean *red*. I do not mean sandy, ginger, rusty or carrot. None of these attractions, however, were his strongest feature. In terms of impact, they were all some way behind a face which boasted truly terrible acne.

I have no idea why this dreaded teenage disease hits some more than others. I do know that the only things I saw Sam eat for the first couple of years I knew him all had icing sugar on them, and that this may have contributed. But whether it was genetic or self induced, or both, it was spectacular. It was industrial strength. It glowed in the dark. But on this day it came a poor second to something else.

I deemed it very important to say nothing. Sam, himself, was studiously strapping his leg pads on, trying to act normally. Avoiding each other's eyes, we engaged in small talk, and then suddenly a few yells from the field signalled that he was due in to bat. He stood up, turned and strode purposely towards the game, during which movement his newly groomed and styled hair never moved. This despite a quite noticeable westerly breeze that had just sprung up, and which was already rippling the shirts and the (un-groomed and un-styled) hair of the rest of us. In fairness to all involved in the project, a Category Five hurricane would not have rippled his hair. It had been combed up and back, and dried and (I think) glued in position.

I never asked him why, and none of the rest of the lads did. The hair-sculpture hung around for about a week, increasingly corroded by the forces of nature and negligence, and then it vanished. But although I didn't ask, I always felt I knew what was behind it. Two weeks earlier, there had been a TV show reminding us of the second anniversary of a rock tragedy. Two years before, at 4.00 p.m. on Easter Sunday, a speeding taxi carrying the touring American rock stars Gene Vincent and Eddie Cochran had crashed, killing the latter. Eddie's memorial album had just been re-released. On it was a picture of the great man. He had hair which was combed up and back, dried and glued.

It is easy to define the impact of rock and roll on teenage Britain in the late fifties and first days of the sixties. You can do it with one word, and have a choice of them at that. 'Massive' does the job quite adequately – or you can stretch to 'seismic'. You can get fancy and call it 'seminal'. Take your pick, or make up your own. It is less easy, however, to track quite *how* it impacted our lives, because it was not like throwing a switch.

In truth, the shenanigans surrounding Bill Haley and his Comets were deceptive. For sure, a few cinemas got wrecked and the seeds were sown but, in reality, when the little fat bugger with the ludicrous kiss-curl plastered on his forehead who fronted the band arrived over in the UK for a tour we knew that this was not the role model required. Teddy Boys appeared for a while, but they were the last vestiges of spivs from the black-market era of wartime and post-war rationing. Their duck's-arse hairstyles were already thinning and their teeth were bad. They were yesterday's men before they got started.

It was to be the true Boomers, those born in the first year(s) of peace, who would really carry the torch for rock music and all it catalysed, and they were still only twelve at this genesis. Well, I was. So it wasn't about Teddy Boys, and in much the same way it wasn't about Elvis or our own British lookalike, Cliff Richard – both of whom were followed by a line of clones on both sides of the Atlantic. Two essential ingredients were not yet fully in place and until they were the rock culture only simmered.

It was not until TV became widespread among the population that the thing went off in everybody's hands. It brought the characters and culture of rock music – and its perpetrators – into every home in a way that hadn't been possible before. It was a double whammy; not only did it make these guys come alive for us, but it also exposed them to our parents. As a result we reinvented the generation gap. It was TV that that really did the trick. Jerry Lee Lewis, you see, for those of who don't remember, played the piano with his arse, and he did it in our front room. Right next to my dad's Rachmaninov records.

At a stroke, right across the land, this created the greatest generation gap, pound for pound, of all time. Before that, these stars had been accessible in the home only on records – which were brilliant, but which could be avoided by parents – and movies, which were artificial crap. By the end of the fifties, we had already become conditioned to Elvis and Cliff morphing into soppy tossers in movies targeted at lobotomized teenage girls.

As TV hit our homes, the first wave of Boomers came of age - i.e. hit their mid teens. We did, anyway. We were a generation that was primed to go off in its own hands. We had a combustive mix of unprecedented purchasing power, indiscipline and exploding hormones. We were sullen. We were unresponsive to support and resistant to control. We desperately needed new role models because the old ones just wouldn't – couldn't – cut it for us. We could already see a world way beyond our parents. Our teachers were wankers and the existing entertainers and recording stars belonged to the arc. Our politicians and public figures seemed to belong to the black and white Movietone News. We had Sir Harold MacMillan and Sir Anthony Eden as Prime Ministers. Or was that Sir Harold Eden and Sir Anthony MacMillan? They looked the same and spoke the same. It wasn't that we didn't give a fuck, it was more that we didn't give a flying fuck; there was no common enemy like Hitler to fight, so that which had united previous generations was missing. So we set about dividing it. Couldn't anybody understand we didn't care about Suez as long as we didn't have to go?

Our role models came in the second wave of American rock stars, and the world was never to be the same again. Little Richard, Jerry Lee Lewis, Chuck Berry, Eddie Cochran and Gene Vincent came over and just got in everybody's face. These were the guys who were lower-profile than Elvis, but without them the Beatle volcano would never have happened. They got us ready for it all. They sang about stuff that made us swear, laugh and yell. TV brought their sweating, demonic faces into the front rooms of all our homes, and they pissed our parents off, and all was well. They married twelve-year-old girls, served jail time and they were *loud*. Their music was not about love and the moon in June; their music was clearly about this mythical thing called shagging that was suddenly looming on all our teenage radar screens. We knew it, they knew it and our parents knew it.

A generation gap is wondrous to behold. It is, of course nothing new. Philip Larkin, in his poem 'This be the Verse', gave it the scientific analysis it had long needed:

> They fuck you up, your mum and dad.
>> They may not mean to but they do.
> They fill you with the faults they had
>> And add some extra, just for you.

So it is always all the fault of the parent(s). They were to blame for this, the broadest, deepest, tallest generation gap in history. All parents generally, and mine specifically, must shoulder the responsibility.

But wait. Larkin goes on:

> ... they were fucked up in their turn
>> By fools in old-style hats and coats,
> Who half the time were soppy-stern
>> And half at one another's throats.

Precisely. Their parents fucked them up, as I in turn have fucked up my own kids. They survived, I survived and my kids have. I'm sure the grandparents did, and I'm sure any grandchildren that come my way will do so to. It's a timeless thing, although each individual gap is finite. The gap is eventually bridged more often than not, usually by physical separation. That our gap was Nobel-worthy in its stature was just a matter of scale and circumstance.

7

They don't mean to

Rational behaviour on both sides of the family table goes off out the window in an industrial-strength generation gap. In the late 1950s I bought my first 45 rpm record, a rather benign sort of rockabilly folk song called 'Tom Dooley', recorded by an American group who went by the name of the Kingston Trio. This coincided with our family purchasing a state-of-the-art radiogram, a piece of furniture about the size of a Bedford van, that combined (wait for it) a radio and gramophone player all in one wooden cabinet. This was then displayed, on legs and with pride, in our family's front (best) room. My father, who had been a senior army officer with the Royal Signals, the high-tech, telecommunications arm of the British army, banned me from playing my new record on the radiogram, using the amazing logic that (are you ready?) such 'rubbish' would *ruin the needle*. It didn't matter that it wasn't a needle anymore, it was now a stylus. And that my record was new and pristine and was made for the new machine, as against his that were made to be played with the equivalent of a rusty nail. Or that throughout history there has not been a case where the content of a record has provided any risk to the mechanics of playing it. This was a generation gap, and logic had no role to play. The good news is that I fought back with even dumber positions on dumber subjects. We could both be highly creative in establishing positions that were completely indefensible.

My dad was a gorgeous man, but he was well positioned to lead one side of the generation gap for the whole of England if they'd have put such a sport in the Olympics. He was a professional army officer and the son of one. Born in the Strand Barracks on the banks of the Shannon in Limerick, Ireland, his early years had all the fun associated with being the son of a British army officer stationed in Ireland around and after the 1916 Easter Uprising. At that stage, he probably (and understandably) developed theories that childhood was not to be enjoyed. As one of nine siblings, you would suspect that his childhood role was to be seen and not heard. You suspect that the debate about his career must have lasted about five seconds, or however long it takes for somebody to say 'You're going in the army.' You suspect that he obeyed or... or... well, you suspect that he just obeyed. In the army, in the 1930s and throughout the war, yours was not to reason why, yours was but to do or die. Again, we are not talking about a James Dean, or somebody who was used to dealing with James Deans.

He had a shitty war. Married just before it started, he was whisked off just a week or so after walking down the aisle, and my mother didn't see him again until early 1945. He was captured by the Japanese as they swept through the Malay Peninsula into Singapore, handing the British Army its most embarrassing and unnecessary defeat in history (all of it – before and since). When his wife did see him again she saw the figure of a man weighing less than a hundred pounds after enjoying the unique form of hospitality shown by the Japanese in their death camps for POWs. You go through and survive this kind of stuff to defend the world that you know, and the values you care about. You do not exist on rice water for over a year to create a world where Jerry Lee can play the piano with his arse in your front room.

Amazingly, God hadn't finished short-changing my dad yet. I arrived in January in the first year of peace (a true, definitive, Boomer), and my arrival was a nightmare for him and my mother. I was premature, weighing in at about the same weight as his war medals, and was not expected to survive the night. I was christened Kevin Barry, after the Irish rebel, by two Irish nurses who then worked their own brand of miracle through the early hours to enable me to live and take on my long term life-mission of putting on another couple of hundred pounds. The crisis passed, and dad kept the Barry (ditching the Kevin). By now he had a job in local government, and he set off to live out the second half of his life in ordered peace.

The ordered peace lasted three and a half years. My mother died of a cerebral haemorrhage on 31 August 1949, and his brave new world collapsed. I celebrated by poking all his war medals, irretrievably it seems, down between the gaps in the floorboards of the building we had all lived in. It is a probable reflection on his contemporary views on the army, war, life and imminent single parenthood that he never sought to get them out.

For a while he and I took on the combined roles of the Ancient Mariner and the albatross as he scrambled to find the right combination of lodgings, looking after me and holding down his job. Then, suddenly, the sun came up for him – disguised as a delightful (and quite stunning) brunette who landed a job as his secretary. They fell in love and married in 1951. He had a new wife; I had a mum. A couple of years later a sister arrived. Technically, they were my half-sister and stepmum. It is a tribute to all the cast that the words 'half' and 'step' have never been mentioned in the decades since.

Once again, he settled down to live out his life in orderly peace. This time he got about twelve years of it, and it was only then interrupted by the ops manual he had brought with him on parenting, built around everything he knew and that he had experienced, being burnt before his eyes.

There was one added factor that didn't help. My new mum came with a father of her own, so I suddenly had two grandparents where none had existed before. The female of the species, my new Nanna, was a grandma from central casting. She was everything a grandma could be. She measured about 4' 10" wherever you put the tape on her, was a marvellous cook and had a lovely, warm personality.

In contrast, my new grandfather, a police inspector by rank, modelled himself some of the more miserable characters in Dickens or Hugo. In fairness, I read the body language early on and kept out of his direct line of fire, but it was his influence on my father that fanned the flames. My father must have felt he had won one of life's bigger lotteries in marrying my stepmother – so if in doubt he shaped his views and behaviour in line with the old-world reactionary who came with the deal. As my W Gene flourished in adolescence and I kept finding new ways to misbehave, I faced my father taking guard with my grandfather as a wicket-keeper. Right behind him. Standing up to the wicket.

We commenced to joust, and continued until I left home at nineteen, confirming one of the irrefutable laws of nature – that no house, however big, can contain a father and a teenage son and a generation gap.

For me it was brilliant. When I did something dumb, I was then only interested in doing something dumber. If (when) I got in trouble, I went

back and got right in more of the same. And all the time, new Boomer milestones came and went. Eddie's Cochran's death only marginally darkened the bright new skies, and we fired another early warning across the bows of the establishment's boat by celebrating the advent of the Twist early in the winter of 1961–2. Such freedom. All you had to do to be a supreme peacock on the dance floor of Ashton's Palais de Dance was to anchor one foot to the ground and proceed to give an imitation of a body with really advanced and terminal Parkinson's Disease. No complicated steps, no treading on your partner's toes. No patronizing looks when you missed a step. You were alone, in your space, doing your own dance thing. There were no rules as to what was good and what wasn't, but you just knew 'good' when you saw it. In spirit, what you were doing on the dance floor was what you did three times a day behind the closed doors of your bedroom, and what the teachers told you would make you blind. Dancing would *never* be the same again.

Between January and September, the four of us – Sam, Geoff, Stuart (Kirky) and I – had our sixteenth birthdays. This was a rite of passage, and we went into it with our eyes wide open. We marched into our immediate future to the rousing metaphoric sound of Tchaikovsky's *1812 Overture*. The shattering explosions which you could hear regularly if you were in our presence, which you might have put down to the cannon associated with the music, were really our hormones going off.

8

Midnight at the oasis

The four of us had started going out together socially earlier in the 1961–2 school year. It wasn't all that regular at the start, and when it happened it would be on a Saturday night, with a pretty rigid formula. We would go home from soccer and have an early supper, then get the bus to Ashton town centre, where we would meet in a pub called the Prince Of Orange. There, for a couple of hours, we would amuse ourselves by breaking the law of the land. We'd drink a few pints of the local Stockport brewery Robinson's bitter ale, some two or three years before it was legal for us to do so.

Drinking alcohol was as much a part of this dying industrial landscape as was soccer. Booze had provided the opiate for the working classes for over two centuries. Earlier in the twentieth century it had caused the new British Minister of Munitions, Lloyd George, to redefine our enemies in the first world war as '...Germany, Austria and drink; and, as far as I can see, the greatest of these deadly foes is drink'. This from a man who, when he eventually became Prime Minister, ran a ménage a trois in Downing Street. Although by the sixties, British per capita consumption of alcohol was only about forty per cent of what it had been at the turn of the century, Manchester was doing its best to prevent further erosion. We took up the challenge enthusiastically.

Underage drinking was barely frowned upon. Bollocks to the law; if you were tall enough to see over the bar counter, that was good enough. Provided it was reasonably controlled, most parents and publicans saw it as a sensible way to introduce the inevitable, rather as the French in-

troduce a glass of wine to the table from an earlier – in their case much earlier – age. We thought little of it. We'd shift a few pints, get cheerfully and mildly pissed, and then sing songs in the backroom of the pub. Wonderful, tasteful melodies that I can recall to this day, such as 'Dinah, Dinah, show us your leg', which was followed by a rousing chorus of 'A yard above your knee'. If we got too loud, we'd be told to bugger off. By about 9.30 we'd be ready to go anyway, targeting our big event of the night, the local Palais de Dance.

About six or eight of us would arrive there, as proceedings (dancing to records and an occasional act) were entering their last hour. There was a bar, but it was expensive so the bulk drinking had been done. This venue and occasion was all about The Chase, and the implausible hunt for a Girl Who Might.

None of them ever actually Would, of course. Even if the building had contained one who Would, it is beyond credibility that any of us would have been able to spot her and then present anything like a plausible case to take advantage of the circumstances. Varying stages of drunkenness diluted any physical attraction we might have had – that had not, indeed, been already removed by our attempts at the latest hair sculptures. Frequent burping and farting poisoned any potentially intimate atmosphere, spiritually and often physically. I have to say that such were the girls we targeted, they were occasionally guilty of this as well; I will not pretend that we were seeking class acts. Dancing also lost some of its appeal as a courting ritual when it was accompanied by ribald yells from your pals hanging over the perimeter balcony, particularly if one was being sick. But we persevered. As I remember, we were all determined to lose our virginities before the Americans reached their stated goal for the 1960s – which was to land a man on Julie Andrews.

We didn't realize it at the time, but, along with a generation of definitive Boomers, we were creating a new science. As we regrouped on Monday morning after one of these, we would, with suitable reluctance and modesty, retell the stories of the later stages of Saturday as we disappeared into the night on our assorted individual end games, most of which involved a solo walk home, long after the last bus had gone. The Monday morning story was, of course, nothing like that. The science we invented, so essential to an imminent generation of politicians and PR folk, was spin-doctoring. The ability to take a grain of truth, and to embellish it beyond belief after an event, with credibility and 'data' to back it up if necessary, belongs, in its entirety, to us.

What Elvis might have looked like if he had owned a donkey jacket

We invented codes of performance when reviewing our imaginary sexual triumphs. 'Upstairs Outside' meant the most basic of base camps had been secured – i.e. the touching of a breast on the outside of whatever clothing the girl was wearing. This was frequently, on account of the generally cold climate, made up of several layers of warm woollens and waterproof garments, so this experience would often reflect an eager hand feeling a barely discernible mound-type shape. Don't knock it; it was wonderful if and when it happened. Our scoring range then climbed up (or down, depending on whether you took these things literally), in theory, to 'Downstairs Inside'. That, I believe, is self-explanatory. I say 'in theory' because that's exactly what it was: academic. I have heard that the Eskimo have fifty different words for snow; in later years, I found that Californians have fifty different words for bread. I am here to tell you that, in the early 1960s, in the north west of England, male teenagers were familiar with fifty different words for female rejection.

On a couple of occasions that winter we made a move further afield into Manchester, where there were several teenage-friendly disco-cum-night clubs. Entry age was officially eighteen, but that proved as easy to overcome as a forward platoon of French infantry. In mid-January 1963, on a cold and bitter night, we paid our first visit to a club called the Oasis, tucked in the back streets behind Manchester Town Hall. Our venue had changed from suburb to city centre, but the ritual and targets were much the same. With a single, everlasting, beer in our hands (beer was even more expensive here than at the Palais), we circled the dance floor looking for dancing girl-couples to 'split' and dance with. Dancing was usually to records, either in between or prior to entertainment acts, and on this occasion a bunch of guys were setting up equipment on the cramped stage.

On one such visit to the Oasis, I was scoring my usual success, and as the lights darkened, I decided I would lean, alone, in what I assumed would seem to be seen as a savagely attractive manner, against a pillar and watch the show. The MC-cum-disc jockey yelled his introduction into the microphone, something about a German band. That seemed strange as Wolvie, one of our group, thought he recognized the drummer as a Liverpool lad. He was right. They were all from Liverpool, about thirty-five miles away. They had just returned from Hamburg, hence the disc-jockey's confusion.

When John Lennon (for it was he) hit the first notes of 'Twist And Shout', two things happened. I forgot all about the really fit looking black girl for whom I had been posing with all the savage sexuality I could muster. I had never been rejected by a black girl before, principally because I'd never approached one, and I'd decided that was the night I was going to make my rejection collection fully multiracial. I have never thought of her again till this moment. The second thing that happened as Lennon full-frontally assaulted every fucking sense we had available, and some we didn't know we had, is that I decided to become a rock singer. This would more than compensate for my failure to become a professional soccer player via the England Schoolboys. If you remember, I missed this life goal because there were several hundred thousand more capable fifteen year olds. Sadly, my New Improved Plan for stardom was also to misfire, as we shall see.

For the record the Beatles made their chart debut with 'Love Me Do' nine months later. They then hit the rest of England, and then the world, with the same impact.

My plan to become a rock star was stillborn immediately and, as it happens, for much the same kind of reason the professional soccer plan failed. We can class both as 'technical difficulties'. After a particularly frustrating sexual experience (or, rather, non-sexual experience, if you get my drift) I was reduced to a languid Doncaster Left-Hander one day. I made a very troubling discovery during this otherwise routine event. While my left hand was so occupied, I found it impossible to break the fingers on a Kit-Kat chocolate biscuit with my right hand. There are those of you who will question my (modern word) 'focus' – how on earth could you dedicate yourself to a DLH while, at the same time, snacking vigorously on a chocolate biscuit? Half a century later, my only defence is that I was a growing lad and always hungry. I changed hands – and attempted the Kit Kat with my left hand. Still no good. With a heavy heart, I realized there and then that my complete inability to do anything in a controlled way with one hand, while the other was creatively occupied, would seriously inhibit guitar playing.

I also found out, around the same time, that Roy Orbison's famed three-and-a-half octave range was greater than mine by *at least* three-and-three-eighths octaves. Then, around the same time, I also discovered I was tone deaf. No range, no coordination and tone deaf. All this was really nothing more than bad timing on my part, because a while later this range of talent would have seen me home dry as a punk rocker, but it was three strikes against me in the early sixties. John, Paul, Ringo and George would hitherto have the field to themselves. Sadly and frustratingly, this particular 'field' included, by my estimate, several hundred million Girls Who Might. Correction – forget Might. These were almost certainly Girls Who Would.

9

School cert

Our accelerating social programme needed funding, and around this time we were all introduced to the idea of work as something you had to do to provide money to do the things you wanted to do. In my case, Sam got me a Saturday morning job in a company where he already had one. It was called G. C. Pies, a manufacturer and distributor of those essentially northern English delicacies, 'meat'-filled pies and pasties. In the last sentence, I put the word meat inside inverted commas deliberately. I worked there. I know what went in them.

These kinds of part-time jobs – and we all had them and many of them – gave us much more than the few shillings needed to fund that evening's activity. For an occasional morning, we would join folk who actually worked in these places for a living. We would be their peers, something that had never happened to us before in our families or schools. We shared jokes with them as equals. We cursed management together. We learned their swear words, they learned ours – which was by no means one-way traffic. We also got to see what life was like at the bottom of the 'casual labour' food chain, with these folk eking out an existence from wage slip to wage slip. And we saw these people treated like dog shit, day in day out, and having no choice but to go back the next day for more of the same. I never checked it out formally with the guys, but I suspect we all started to shape a determination that we would find something better than this in life. And some longer-term seeds were also sown. In future years, I would never allow myself to conveniently forget that life can be just fucking awful at the furthest point away from the boardroom chandeliers – and I can find no politer or more accurate way of expressing it than that.

My Saturday morning pie-making skills became legendary. This was a company untroubled by quality standards or almost any safety rules, and who had invented 'zero-tolerance' for its workforce forty years before it was to become the party idea of the 1990s. Depending on what mood I was in, and the technical accessibility of my morning's position on the pie-filling assembly line, I would occasionally pass the whole morning by attempting to blow my nose in every fiftieth pie that passed. That worked best in the winter months when I had a cold. I cannot bring myself to tell you what one of us put in an historic meat and potato pie on one dark, foul day that winter. I can only tell you it may have been the first – and only – attempt a pie cloning.

I never achieved my ambition at G. C. Pies, which was spending a morning as a jelly pourer. When the pork pies had partly cooled after baking, it was the job of a favoured employee to fill a large tea-pot with some sort of glutinous jelly stuff, and pour a little into each individual pie through a small hole left in the pastry lid. I was never favoured enough to be given the kettle. It is probably just as well; I could have done stuff with that opportunity that would have wiped out whole suburbs. By the by, I hope that puts paid to a stupid rumour which has grown as to the true reason for these holes in the top of pork pies. The real reason is for the aforesaid jelly entrance and not so that Lancashire men can carry a six-pack back from the chippy.

With all these extraneous excitement, my *raison d'être* of the time – schooling (remember?) – continued to suffer. Academically, Sam, Geoff and Kirky managed to maintain their progress, despite suddenly having to drag me along like a truck. I did start getting them into more trouble as they collectively began to substitute for the departed Gill in my plans to full-frontally attack everything at the school and what it stood for. They were, however, showing promising signs of being able to do this on their own.

As we moved into spring, the dreaded GCEs raised their head again. For those three it was to be the first time, and they were all forecast to do well enough to return for the pre-university sixth form course. For me, a no-hoper, it was also to be the first time, having forfeited it the previous year and stayed down. As I was clearly going to fail and leave, Exeley kindly agreed to deflect enough British taxpayer's money to let me take the exam in the seven subjects I had taken on the curriculum.

At home, my parents were increasingly bewildered. I was clearly bright in some areas, but my school reports and recorded academic performances were just elongated and coded articulations of the words 'twat' and 'prat'. At one memorable parent's evening in school, when my father and I reached the front of a short queue in front of my form master, he (the form master) suddenly realised who was in front of his table and blanched. There was a long pause, then he (the form master again, and I'm not inventing this) began pulling on his hair. And I mean pulling. Eventually he croaked – and I'm not inventing 'croaked' either – 'He gets in *my hair*'. My father, wisely, decided to end the evening right there and then. It was a long drive home.

In their eyes I had all the advantages that caring and aspiring parents can bring to the cause of the academic performance of a child. In their eyes it was impossible for anybody to misplay such a God-given hand of cards. But by the summer of 1962 they had come out of denial, and accepted that I was to be out on the streets, unqualified, at sixteen.

We began to think of possible jobs, ones that might get me to an eventual set of qualifications via the 'vocational' route. We went through the idea of becoming articled to an accountant (my input? Fuck that), or the army (double-fuck that). Eventually mum came up with something than attracted me for all the wrong reasons. She had an old friend in the Merchant Navy, and apparently you could join as an apprentice navigating officer at sixteen, and rise through the ranks. I knew nothing of the life, and didn't give a monkey's about the game plan or the future. But it would get me out of Ashton and expose me to whole nations of exciting foreign Girls Who Would, so I began the application process. Miraculously, I passed the first stage which was a strict eyesight test, which would have come as an enormous shock to Holy Joe had I bothered to tell him.

The downside to this plan was that I had to get two of my seven GCEs, which was a crap shoot. So the start date was fixed as September, a month after the results were published. I left school in July, never to return. I wasn't angry on the day, or sad, or happy, or excited, or scared. I remember feeling numb. I remember being cold, and it was a lovely sunny day.

Two of the houses in our secluded avenue were owned by Whitbread, a dominant British brewing company of the time. They had no brewery in this heavy beer-drinking market, so they shipped bulk beer in from other parts of the country, and had a packaging plant locally. Here, bulk beer would be bottled or put in metal kegs, and then sent in pallet loads to distribution depots who would then deliver the individual orders to pubs and off-licences (liquor stores). By courtesy of one of neighbours who occupied one of those company houses I got a job for the summer at the packaging plant.

This was a different league than the pie shop. I had to join a union (for the one and only time in my life), and I was introduced to the fatuous battle that dominated British industry for most of the next two decades: organized labour versus management. Here I learned that everything I did was to be at a determined pace, pre-agreed by all parties so that it would generate guaranteed overtime at time-and-a-half pay rates. Here I learned that the union had negotiated a beer allowance of five pints per man per day, which you *must* drink. The latter was peer-group custom and practice, rather than constitutional – but it often meant you would then go back to work after lunch, when you'd maybe downed two or three of them, and drive a fork lift truck, likely as not with a full pallet of beer on it. Even better, that pallet was often twenty feet in the air, above workers unprotected by hard hats.

As part of this apprenticeship, I learned of man's inhumanity to man through cruel jokes. I filled gaping holes in my inadequate formal education. I learned that if you taught a Polish guy who spoke no English to say 'fuckov' every time the foreman came round, it was truly, and I mean *truly*, hilarious. I learned that if you knew a guy who came into the locker room before his shift, and that every morning that guy disappeared into the same lavatory cubicle and had a monstrous and smelly crap, that if you lifted the toilet seat beforehand, and took clear polythene and stretched it across the top of the toilet, and then put the lid back down, that the results of such a plan would be such that your stomach ached from laughter for two days.

The bad news was that I loved it. The money was (relatively) tremendous, and I could fund several nights a week drinking and pursuing this legendary, and increasingly obsessive, shagging thing.

I loved the beer, and with five pints a day plus a few nights out, my skinny frame filled out. I stopped getting knocked about at soccer, and began to fill my jacket out. I was lifting full crates and kegs of beer all day, and on into the night if the overtime was available. Strange bulges appeared on my upper forearms. Astonishingly, a single long hair appeared on my chest, which has since been joined by eight more – each one arriving, like clockwork, at steady six year intervals.

I knew it wasn't right for life, but right there, right then, you could have left me alone for a couple of years and my ship would have righted itself. I was certainly beginning to go off the idea of the Merchant Navy. In late August, I was, unusually, outside in the dispatch yard. I was on top of a wagon, helping to sheet (rope) it up. Somebody yelled my name, and I looked up to see the shift supervisor walking over to me. He was recognisable by the fact he had about six biros in the outside breast pocket of his light brown overall coat – which signalled the fact that part of his job description involved paperwork. He was accompanied by my father. He (my father) was recognisable by his (usual) very smart jacket, collar and tie, all of which stood out like a sore thumb in that place. My first, natural, response was to mentally re-run my activities of the last week or so, analysing the potential Disastrous Consequence factor of any transgressions (you know, angry fathers of embarrassed daughters sort of thing). But nothing came to mind. I strengthened myself to face the onslaught because this was obviously something out of the ordinary. For him to leave work, find his way to the plant and seek me out mid shift, was a one-off. I was obviously in deep doo-doo.

As he got nearer, I saw he was smiling. Hell, no – no, he wasn't, he was red faced and *laughing*. He was holding his hands up in front of his face, with a bunch of fingers extended. 'You've passed them all. All seven!'

Either through a complete lack of interest (possibly), or a sense of foreboding (probably), my mind was empty on the subject of exam results. That day was apparently Results Day. To this day, I have no idea how my father got them, but got them he had. I had passed the lot.

I don't think either of us said anything else.

I loved my dad (as the Americans say) from soup to nuts. Sure, we had a pissing contest in my teens, and it was to get worse, much worse. But if love is about being happy *for* someone occasionally, I loved him all right. I actually didn't give a thought to what it meant for me for quite a while, I really was so happy to see him beaming.

I quit work early that day. No overtime, no five pints (I usually saved all mine for the end of the day). I got home and phoned Sam, Geoff and Kirky. They had all triumphed as well, Sam spectacularly so.

The family supper that night was fun. It was only towards the end of it that the obvious became so. I would not be joining the Navy, *I would be going back to school*. The four of us would be entering the sixth form.

As I drifted to sleep that night, I wondered what Exeley was thinking. It must have passed through his mind that Rambo Lite would just not go away. Rambo Lite was heading back into town. What he (Exeley) didn't know was that he (Rambo Lite) was bigger and stronger. And he had a whole new hair on his chest.

10

Cuba libre

In October 1962, an asthmatic urban guerrilla with a splotchy beard urged his boss to urge, in turn, his bosses to take the planet to the brink of the first potential force-ten clusterfuck since World War Two.

Che Guevara was the guerrilla. It was a few years after his Cuban triumph. It was still some years before an opportunistic photographer captured him in a pose (and with a beret) that would eventually see him adorn the bedroom walls of a goodly portion of a generation of the world's students. Fidel Castro was his boss. A man with a much more powerful beard. Their own 'bosses' were, in turn, thousands of miles away in Moscow. They were lead by an unstable, bombastic mouth-breather called Kruschev. No beard for him; in fact, no cranial hair at all.

Heading across the North Atlantic was a cargo of nuclear warheads, bound for Cuba, where they would join some already in place. The latter were already pointed strategically at Uncle Sam's groin.

The 'West', as it had come to be known, figure-headed at the time by a young US President who looked more like Bobby Vinton than he did a Global Leader, was having the opposite of an orgasm. Whatever that might be called[3]. President John F. Kennedy, aided by his brother Robert, and possibly their family cat, seemed resolute. The convoy would be stopped at all costs. Over a weekend the world – apparently – held its collective breath.

---

3   I've thought about this long and hard. I think the technical term for the opposite of an orgasm might be a 'went'.

I say 'apparently' because I've read about it since. At the time, although I was made aware of it, and of its apocalyptic potential significance, the whole episode couldn't force itself into the top ten of my Things to Concern Myself With. I was too busy refusing to take one of the many chances that were being offered to me to become an adult.

As the planet teetered, that very same weekend I was in a tiny north Yorkshire hamlet called Muker, along with Sam and the other two. The four of us were guests at the weekend cottage of our school form master, Mark Gibbs – a well-meaning, deeply religious pursuer of lost causes. We were in our second month back at school after our 'O' Levels. We were in the lower sixth form.

Entering the sixth form in an English 1950s all-boys grammar school signalled a change in the learning climate. It was somewhat akin to a modern professional golf tournament, in that by qualifying to play in the weekly tournament itself meant you were supposed to be the cream of the golfing crop. The grammar school was the same for school life. Then, the 'O' level exams weeded out the also-rans, rather like the golf tournament 'cut' on a Friday night. Like the golfers who made it to the weekend, sixth-formers were the serious players. They were essentially destined for university, or at least to have a crack at it. With this in mind the scholastic subjects covered were reduced to three, grouped in either 'arts' or 'science', and you had two years to prepare for an 'advanced' level test in them. Real success would qualify you for further specialism at university.

Hand in hand with the new curriculum came a new, nauseating, establishment tokenism. It was as though the passing of a sixteenth birthday signalled that a slightly changed, but still tightly controlled, attitude was needed. Something that signalled that the sixth form was more of a partnership. We'd got rid of 'them'; now it was all 'us'. Young adult to mature adult, but still adult to adult. Dinky little privileges and patronizing practices started to become noticeable. This is obviously how it worked for previous generations, and was a cornerstone in the rites of passage to maturity. We were expected to accept this mass lobotomy and respond with suitable goodwill, maturity and gratitude.

Bollocks to all that. This was really fertile ground for the W Gene.

What had changed is that most of this generation went through their sixteenth birthdays as though they were going through the sound barrier. What was different was that we had been the equivalent of a previous generation's sixteen when we were twelve, and that was history. The sight or sound of any adult coming out of their corner to meet us half way across the ring just brought hoots of derision. They wanted adults? We became children again. Fun-O.

The Muker weekend set the tone for the whole of my sixth form. Mark Gibbs had a long history of being a form master for first-year sixth-formers. He was, until then, made for it. A serious looking man, quiet of manner, he cared enough about his responsibilities to oversee the birth of a gaggle of new wannabe-adults to invest a lot of his spare time in the cause. He was also a big cheese in the World Council of Churches, and this gave him a sort of statesman's credibility in our small world. It was one of his jobs to introduce us to the idea of seriously de-bating world issues. He seemed to want to know our opinions on stuff that was out there way beyond the search for Girls Who Might.

He had invested in a two-up, two-down cottage high up (geographi-cally and altitudinally) in the Yorkshire Dales, and part of his modus operandi was to take his lower-sixth formers up there for a weekend, in groups of three or four at a time. As we four were by now inseparable, and had already run foul of a few rules, he took on the challenge of get-ting us up there. Unstated goal: he was going to sort these bastards out early.

On the Friday night, he picked us up in his car and we journeyed up from Manchester. He was very pensive. Perhaps he had good cause to be. By then 1400 US nuclear bombers were on DEFLON 2 alert. For the record, DEFLON 5 was peace; DEFLON 1 was war. As our contribution to the crisis, we hilariously tried, as a chorus, to pronounce, as words, all the letter groupings on the car number plates that went past. This ef-fectively and annoyingly (for him) drowned out the latest bulletins on the crisis coming over the car radio. He realized then that this was to be a long weekend. He got mad at us during the journey, something we had never seen him do before. We decided we wanted more.

At sixteen, it would be wrong to say we were addicted to gambling. But not by much. Small-scale betting was part of the working class way of life, usually done through the football pools, or at the weekend in the off-track betting shops that adorned most high streets. For generations, a small flutter had provided some relief in a grim way of life, and occa-sionally (via a big Pools win) a ticket to leave it all behind.

The varieties of card games that enabled betting were almost infinite, and often took up much of a working-weekday lunch time break or an evening in the pub. We were already enthusiasts, particularly for the latter. Money was teenager-tight, stakes were small, but neither of those diluted the fervour of the card schools. Way before we had boarded the car for Muker, we had scoped the weekend ahead as a minimally interrupted card school. DEFLON would have to wait. It got a wee bit out of hand.

The first evening, to our surprise, Gibbs took us to the pub. Remember, we were sixteen, two years under the legal drinking age, and here was a pillar of the establishment, who was also a big cheese in the Godsworld Themepark, being an accomplice in a bit of law breaking. 'Twas not what it seemed. Underage drinking was no big deal in this part of the world, and we were already quite hardened beer drinkers. He also knew he was taking no risks with this grand gesture, stuck away in this poxy little village; it was part of his tokenism. As we sat down with our half pints of ale (halves, for Christ's sake) he kept harping on about the end of the world.

Saturday dawned, and two things were evident at breakfast. First, that we hadn't slept much – it had been a long card school. Second, nobody had blinked in the big pissing contest going on in the Atlantic. 'Black Saturday' dragged on, with everything getting worse on every front, including our master's mood and temper.

When the world went to bed that night, many doubted there would be a tomorrow. Down in our shared bedroom (basically the ground floor of the cottage) we decided that – as this might be our last one – we'd have the mother of all card schools. On and on it went. It got noisier. Finally, one incredible hand blew the lid off the whole thing as it built up and up, finally leaving me and Kirky sweating at each other over (our equivalent of) a king's ransom. The other two joined in by howling alternate support and abuse. Sometime in the wee early hours, Kirky paid to see my hand. The bastard deity who oversees these things had put two of the top three possible hands out in the same deal, and he had the winner.

Bollocks to Cuba. This was the end of civilization and the four of us were yelling and swearing and laughing like, well, sixteen year olds. Suddenly, a thump from upstairs told us we had woken our Kraken, and we heard his footsteps heading south.

We scrambled like World War Two pilots – only in our case into sleeping positions. I was in a sleeping bag on a couch which converted into a bed. We awaited the entrance. 'For fuck's sake, the light's still on,' came a muffled cry from somebody, and so it was.

I was nearest the switch. I stood up in my sleeping bag. I had no time to get out of it. I set off towards the wall by the door, the ancestral home of the appropriate light switch. I hopped in my sleeping bag like some demented parent at a school sports day trying the sack race. Eventually I got to it, and turned it off. In the dark, I turned to hop back to my bed. I then heard the magic sound of my convertible bed reconverting into a couch – courtesy of my one of close and supportive buddies who had reached over and slammed it shut.

The door opened and the light went back on. In stormed our hero. He was greeted by a scene that would be tough to recreate, even given three months notice and the availability of the Marx brothers. I was three feet into the room, standing inside my sleeping bag, which I was holding vertically by clamping it under my armpits. I had tears streaming down my face, but I was, gentle reader, *feigning sleep*. On various other bed-like facilities were three bodies, facing away from the door, in assorted horizontal poses, shuddering quite violently. The shuddering was not to do with fear, pain, or illness, or cold; it was to do with supressed laughter. The noise was not what you would expect from four deep-sleeping teenagers.

Gibbs drew himself up to his full height (not much, really) and set off on some lecture. None of which I can remember, apart from the bottom line. As early as was possible, given Sunday train times, we would be packed off home on the morrow. Our parents would be informed, as would the headmaster. He then did one of these sweeping exits.

We went quietly. Later on the Sunday, after we had gone, Kruschev blinked. His words echoed around the planet: 'In order to save the world we must retreat'.

I celebrated by having my sixth form privileges (mainly a tie) withdrawn permanently.

11

Saturday night's all right

We didn't have a world to save, so we didn't. In fact, quite the opposite. The Muker incident hardened our school reputation, generally, and mine specifically. So we kept on attacking.

It was very hard for the parental and school Establishment to put a fire blanket on this attitude and activity. They didn't understand why there was aggression when there didn't seem to be the need for any. They didn't understand that, when there were so many things, good and bad, going on in the new world, a generation could be so self-centred and insular. They didn't understand why we were only interested in card schools when the threat of being bombed into a sticky black paste seemed horribly close.

Of course we knew the stakes. Since the Aldermaston marches 1958, and the growing presence of the inverted Y of the CND movement, the issues around the nuclear threat and the case for disarmament (wanted by many to be unilateral) had been front-centre news. You'd have had to be deaf, dumb and blind not to be aware of it all. But it was of no interest to us. It was never articulated, but the lifelong Boomer maxim was already alive and well: somebody else deals the cards of life. Good, bad or indifferent, we'll play them. Meanwhile, we've got other things to do.

What many people miss in analysing the zeitgeist of the early sixties is that the icons of profound change – and I mean *profound* – had not arrived yet. Elvis and James Dean had been, but by now they were old hat. Elvis was already a Hollywood and army sell-out and much of the other current music was candy-ass. The first wave of breakthrough icons – Jerry Lee Lewis, Chuck Berry, Eddie Cochran, Gene Vincent et al – were fading (or dead) by 1963.

In literature the Angry Young Men, heralded by John Osborne's Jimmy Porter (*Look Back In Anger, 1956*) and John Braine (*Room at the Top, 1957*), were like Elvis. To use a baseball expression, they were the set-up pitchers.

The main breakthrough agents were, of course, still learning their trade in Hamburg's cellar bars. But while they were doing that, a very powerful silver-medal winner was already kicking the door down. At least, that that was the impact for me, for us and the industrial northwest of England.

Alan Sillitoe's 1958 novel *Saturday Night and Sunday Morning* was turned into a film by Karl Reisz in the early sixties. It was set in our homeland, and starred Albert Finney as Arthur Seaton, who juxtaposed the alienating, aimless banality of blue-collar weekday working life with wild weekends of booze and sex. Arthur inhabited a responsibility-free zone. He was lobotomized in the week, and on Saturday and Sunday he spent everything he had earned, saved nothing, and shagged and drank for England. There was *nothing else* on his radar screen. It was only many, many years later I realized just how good Finney was, but at the time it was Arthur Seaton who hit me like a heat-seeking missile.

We tried, oh, how we tried. School became our equivalent of Arthur's weekday factory. We did the minimum possible to get through, we were sullen, aggressive and annoying where possible. We fought when we were trodden on. We made it to each weekend.

It was the weekend bit that kept falling short. The drinking bit was OK, there was lots of beer. We also managed to mix and match our teenage wardrobes in a way that pissed our parents off. Lots of black, with touches of white. Tight trousers. At least this enabled us to give off a few Arthur-type signals. But this Shagging for England bit was a long time coming.

As 1962 ended, it had been four and a half years since I had experienced my first unchaste kiss. That spectacular blend of science and art launched a lifetime of addiction to the practice. The girl involved was called Janet; I haven't seen her since, but I remember the time, place and thrill as if it were half an hour ago. It happened in surroundings that did not do anything like justice to golden glow it created – the cheap seats in Ashton's scruffy cinema. When we locked lips I took right off on an out-of-body journey which lasted – what? – maybe thirty seconds. During that period the area around where I think my heart is was hit by a truck at least fifty times. It gave me an erection that lasted longer than Yuri Gagarin's jaunt in space. The whole thing has at least an equal ranking in my history.

Further sexual progress since then, however, had been *très* constipated. A lot more kisses, lots of Upstairs Outside, lots of talk, lots of spindoctoring and a million white lies. But never the real thing. Luckily, help was on the way. The equivalent of Seventh Cavalry was just outside our canyon, and ready to come to our rescue.

We were aware that something was happening that might help our chances and increase the local inventory of Girls Who Might. Something called the 'Sixties' (subtitled the 'sexual revolution') had erupted in London, about two hundred miles to the south of us. By all accounts, it had left the capital, I think by bus, and was heading north, like one of those red blotches on a modern TV weather map that show the progression of a storm system. Liverpool and Manchester generally, and me oh-so-specifically, were ready to receive it. With open arms, an open heart and an open fly. Jesus, by this time I was ready to die for the cause.

12

Gimme that thing

Those of you familiar with Philip Larkin's work will know that sex was invented in 1963, between the de-banning of D. H. Lawrence's *Lady Chatterley's Lover* and the release of the Beatles' first album *Please Please Me*.

In my case, that reflects pinpoint accuracy.

As the spring of that momentous year approached, I found myself in the best physical shape of my young life. I was ready for the tests ahead. Lots of beer, an appetite like a horse and a very busy sporting calendar had combined to bulk up my spindly physique. The enhanced calorie traffic was still of a mind to find its resting place in the parts of my body where it worked to my advantage. Oh, happy days.

At the start of the winter, the legendary Snipe boy's soccer team had broken up, with Sam leaving to play in a senior amateur league. More importantly for the purposes of keeping the team alive, Sam Senior had decided that the departure of his son signalled the time for him to hang up his bladder bag. Kirky also went on to greater things. Through a couple of other school mates, I got a Saturday game with a team based in Clayton, a less-than-leafy suburb clustered round a chemical plant just east of Manchester itself. I set out again in the pursuit of my soccer fame and fortune.

Such ambitions received a blow early on in the school term.

Being in the sixth form, and ceasing being 'under sixteen', I qualified to play for one of the two senior rugby teams the school put out every Saturday morning. Somehow or other, Sam and Kirky's outstanding soccer prowess (and the 'good name' this indirectly reflected on the school) gave them dispensation on a Saturday, and they avoided being picked to play rugby. I assumed the same would apply to me – for a different reason. I was crap at rugby.

The team sheets for Saturday went up on the school notice board on Thursday mornings, and very early on in the school year, on one such Thursday, I was told with much hilarity, by about fifty of my fellow pupils, that I was playing on the following Saturday morning. I sought out the notice board with a sense of dread. There it was – and I was listed as full back for the second team for an away match at another grammar school in Manchester. I was to report to school on the Saturday at virtually the normal weekday school time. The early start enabled us to get the team bus, which got us to our destination in time for a 10.00 a.m. kick off. This jeopardized my ability to get back in time to play my afternoon soccer match, let alone my ability to actually contribute anything physical to the second game. It also removed Saturday morning money-earning potential, a big blow to the cash flow deemed necessary to pursue Girls Who Might. A plan was needed.

I invented a new rugby position. It is one which I do not believe existed before my brief rugby career, and one I have not heard reprised. It became known as the non-playing full back. I took the field on a wet, windy, dirty Saturday morning, and left it after eighty muddy minutes *without a stain on my shorts or jersey*. Wherever the ball was, I wasn't. If there was action, there was an absence of yours truly. We lost heavily.

Exactly the same script was followed the following week, this time for a home match. I believe the defeat was heavier.

It was in the company of a high degree of optimism that I approached the school notice board on the following Thursday. It was quickly shattered. The bastards had picked me again, only this time with a twist. After my name, in brackets, was the word 'captain'.

With the wisdom of the years I can only reflect that this might have been a flailing, final attempt to salvage me – 'I know, let's try and give him some responsibility' – and get me across some sort of drawbridge and into the cultural fortress of the school. Whatever the motive, I was having none of it. Up over the parapet popped the W Gene's head.

I was blessed with an opportunity to shove their scheme up their bums on my debut as captain. It was another away match in the Manchester area, and the weather and pitch topography combined to give me my chance. The wind was howling, and it blew straight up and down the pitch. I won the toss and decided to play the first half with the advantage of the gale at our backs. It was a measure of our inadequacy that, by half time, we had only achieved an 11–0 advantage. Each school team had a master appointed as a coach/manager, and, despite the encouraging noises of our guy, there wasn't one of us in the shivering half-time huddle that didn't anticipate a final score in the region of 11–186 in the opposition's favour. Apart from me.

I had seen the route to our salvation in an incident during the first half. The rules of rugby had not yet been amended to prevent you kicking the ball into touch from anywhere on the pitch. I had done so once early on in the game. Alongside the touchline there was a fence, and the ball sailed high over both. It transpired that this school had a low-budget rugby programme, and this was the only ball available. One of their players had to climb the fence to retrieve it, and it took nearly ten minutes as it got lost in about three acres of heather and gorse. The incident was noted by Captain Fantastic (me) for further use.

The second half was less than a minute old when we were already pinned down defending our line. That endless first minute still had life left in it when my first kick for touch cleared the side line, and the fence, by about thirty feet. The relief was like Mafeking. It took the planned time for one of them to climb the fence and retrieve the ball. The minute it was back in play, I kicked it over the fence again. The home school traditionally provided the referees for these occasions, and this time the ball sailed high into no-man's land accompanied by signs of clear annoyance from the opposition and an entreaty to 'play the game' from their referee. Bollocks to that.

I must have put it over the fence a dozen times before the whole thing imploded. Each one was accompanied by increasing fury from the opposition and referee, embarrassment from our school coach who was on the side line, and delight from the other fourteen on my side. The game threatened to spill over into Sunday. Finally, the referee called me over. His face was white, and he gave me a speech about never having come across anything like it in a lifetime of schoolboy rugby. Then he sent me off.

No matter, the damage had been done. The fourteen survivors of our heroic team hung on like leeches without their intrepid captain, and we ran out 11–3 winners. It was a sign of just how far I was away from understanding the plot that I thought that would be the end of it.

You would have thought that I had eaten Exeley's first born. Our Headmaster from Hell had me in his office at ten past nine on the following Monday morning, and gave me an astonishing speech. As I watched him, I remember questioning (silently) how anybody could rant and rave so loudly, for so long, *and never swear once*. It was impressive, but what followed was less so. I got ten of the best. Ten! Top end of the range! It was the only game the second team won all year, and I led them to victory. I got caned for my efforts. It was, I think, the last ever caning at Audenshaw Grammar School. The sore arse was worth it. They closed the drawbridge and left me outside. As part of that, I never played rugby for the school again, and could carry on with Saturday soccer unimpeded.

The latter was important not only to do justice to the soccer team, but to avoid unnecessary hiccoughs in one version of the Saturday night courting ritual. On one of the occasions I played twice (rugby in the morning, soccer in the afternoon) during the day on the Saturday, I had a date at the cinema in the evening. At a crucial moment in the proceedings (mine, not the movie's) I got violent leg cramps as a result of my earlier doubled-up sporting effort. You can trust me on this: when you get leg cramps in the cinema there is only one way to go. That way is upwards. When you reach a standing position, you become frozen, like a stone statue. Any movement brings agony, so you remain in that exact position for what seems to you a nanosecond while the blood clots disengage. Apparently it is actually quite a bit longer than that, and this creates a problem for others. You become almost as popular with a) your date and b) those immediately behind you as you would have been if you had kicked their only rugby ball out of sight and reach.

Another vehicle which indicated much promise for the pursuit and landing of Girls Who Might emerged around this time: the teenage party. These followed a fairly standard structure – a set of parents would be either foolish enough to allow it while they were out for the evening or, more likely, they would be away for the weekend on a trip to relatives and were daft enough to trust their teenage son/daughter to 'look after the house' for the first time. After a few beers in the Prince of Orange, a quick trip to the off-licence armed you with a seven pint take-away can of beer, an invention that was just hitting the shops with the party market in mind.

When you arrived at the house in question, you would dump the beer off in the kitchen as your contribution, and slide with cool nonchalance into the main room, where what seemed like eight thousand teenagers would already be in the early throes of their own individual mating rituals. This involved travelling in a circuit with four quite clearly defined stops on it. You started with the record player (which was invariably a Dansette), where you would loudly illustrate to anyone within hearing distance your deep and intimate knowledge of what was on the cutting edge of pop music. This was done by the judicial dropping of gold nuggets of information – perhaps a sound-bite of a value judgment on the Beatles' not yet released new record that you had managed to hear somehow late at night on Radio Luxembourg. All lies, but strangely effective.

Your second stop on this tour was the bathroom. Bearing in mind what was possibly ahead, it was imperative that your hair, which had been teased into place with about two pounds of Brylcreem, kept its formidable shape. A quick comb, a couple of cool, leering poses in the mirror, and you were ready for the next stage.

The next stop was the kitchen. Food was not a big item at these events, and any that had been prepared had long disappeared before you arrived. But there was a serious challenge in the kitchen – which was to make sure that you drank a lot more beer than you brought with you.

Thus armed, you sauntered back into the main room for the key stop on the circuit. The pick-up. On several previous laps you would have identified your target and, with any luck, might have had an encouraging smile or wink in response to your cool leer. The girls always hunted in packs and the trick was to use sheepdog-like tactics and split one from her group without either the victim or the group noticing. This was not as hard as it sounds. They were there for the same thing.

The party population eventually paired off. About nine o'clock the music slowed and the lights went off. There then began a period which consisted of an activity called 'necking'. This was a ridiculously undescriptive title, as the neck was the focus of nothing. What necking did involve, unless you were lucky enough to land the settee or bold enough to get a share of one of the upstairs beds (which you shared with about thirty coats and possibly three other couples), was enormous discomfort. This was partly due to the fact that, if you were the male of the couple, your erection, which would have been a thing of beauty in an open-air situation, was hampered by your suddenly way too tight trousers. It was also partly due to the fact that your romantic tryst was occasionally interrupted by somebody's foot banging your ear.

I learned three lessons from such parties. I learned that, in the pursuit of Girls Who Might, the Best can be the enemy of the Available. This particular lesson stood me in great stead later in business life.

I learned, also, that I had, on occasion, strange powers. About this time, just as the Beatles had breached the wall, about two million four-man Beatle-wannabe groups appeared behind them. Every city had it own collection, but they were not yet famous enough to abandon their roots, and would frequently join in the social life in between infrequent bookings. In Manchester we had the Hollies, Freddie and the Dreamers, Herman's Hermits and Wayne Fontana. Widespread fame still awaited them all, but they had all achieved some local celebratory status by then. Wayne Fontana was backed, at that time, by a group called the Jets, later to become the Mindbenders, and who then spawned several other groups. All five of them turned up at a party in Denton one Saturday. By about nine o'clock, I had done about six circuits, and there was no doubt as to my company for the next couple of hours. I had received six increasingly encouraging signs during my laps, and one more trip to the lav and a beer top-up was all that stood between me and her, and a delightful, if uncomfortable, period of constrained passion. Suitably primed, I moved in – only to find that Wayne Fontana, the man himself, had stepped in to reap the benefit of my spadework while I had been filling my beer glass. He stole my woman. The bastard. There and then I put the Curse of Gibbo on him, and what followed was extraordinary. Within a few years he had lost his hair and turned decidedly loopy. Clearly, this is an awesome power, and it is one I have disciplined myself to use sparingly over the years. But if you are upset by anything in this book, and you meet me on the street, and you are of a mind to do something about it, you would do well to remember poor Wayne.

Third lesson? Parties also gave me an early warning about life's potential cruelties. They occasionally combined actors and scripts in a way that illustrated that it was pointless to go on. That death was not only a pleasant, but also the only option. That you must end it all. That you must go home quietly and throw yourself off the top of your record collection.

A girl called Sue was my target. Her reputation as a Girl Who Wouldn't was hinted at in her nickname: Ironblouse. No matter, she was a delightful lass, and I was seriously in love with her, albeit from a distance. I had decided that Geoff Barratt's party was to be the scene of my great breakthrough. In fairness, I believe I got a hint of an encouraging smile from her on my third lap and, with the clock just a couple of minutes short of 21.00 hours, I moved in, military style, for the kill. To my absolute delight, and to every other guy's absolute astonishment, I was warmly received. So warmly, in fact, that as the lights went down, it was she who manoeuvred us onto the only settee available. The first kiss left me in no doubt: Ironblouse was melting. I launched into a second one like an Olympic long jumper forced to do so without his run up, and something beyond belief happened. *Her hand sought my groin.* It (the hand) grabbed my 'nads and started, well, what can only be described as a kneading exercise. Then, she grabbed my whatsit, which by this stage was eminently grabbable, and began pulling and pushing and twisting and jerking. My eyes began to water, some of which was due to passion, but most of which was down to pain. No matter, this was it. This was going to be the night. As the kneading went on, increasing in vigour, my kisses (in response) assumed a physical intensity that within a very short time had her eyes watering in sympathy. Apart from her hyperactive hand, her body seemed strangely rigid.

Really low moments in your life are interesting phenomena. They become frozen tableaux, and never leave you. Every detail remains crystal clear, and is never to be diluted, or even offset, by memories of compensating triumphs. Such a moment occurred when the lights were suddenly switched on by my mates at about ten past nine on that fated evening. Sue and I were locked in the joint pose I have described above. With one very important exception. The hand that was doing the passionate damage to my groin was not actually hers. It belonged to Wolvie, my pal from Ashton Grammar school, who, encouraged by the rest of the buggers, had crawled on the floor, in the dark, around the back of the settee, then made his way along the side of it – from whence he could just reach round, and up, and grab my bollocks. Which he proceeded to knead with the aforementioned enthusiasm. Sue's hand, which I had mistakenly thought was doing the delightful damage, was actually trapped painfully under her body, which by this time had assumed the properties of a roll of lino. A roll of lino, that is, which had eyes that had narrowed and glazed over. Interestingly, from a scientific point of view, her body had also assumed the temperature of a roll of lino.

My misery remained, but salvation was to arrive shortly. As Manchester's bleak wet winters eventually inched, with sullenness and a lack of grace, into pale, watery, springs, there was an annual event to mark the transition. The river valley between Ashton and Audenshaw, poetically called Daisy Nook, each year hosted a Spring Fair over a long weekend, an event and location immortalised by L. S. Lowry. The invariable inclement weather and high water table always combined to give the ground the same properties as a northern French battlefield in 1914, and the temporary men's lavatories were a location which was essential to a) avoid and b) keep downwind. Even back in 1963, the whole event seemed a century out of date, featuring a three-legged lamb and a bearded lady among its prize exhibits. You could also take on some 'ex-heavyweight boxing champion' for a shilling, and if you knocked him over in a three-minute round you won five pounds. More importantly, however, for a long weekend, it added a new dimension to the boy meets girl routine. And right in the epicentre of Philip Larkin's defined period, I struck gold.

Still recovering from the death-by-embarrassment of Barratt's party, I needed a high profile morale booster. It came in the form of Kate, a tall, rather gangly, but pretty hairdresser. The set-up circumstances have long gone from my memory, but somehow I ended up talking with her on one of the few dry bits of ground at Daisy Nook. We were suddenly and surprisingly alone. It became clear very quickly that this was something different – an older woman. By that I mean twenty-two. I badly needed a trophy of this gravitas and magnitude, and gave it my best pitch. She agreed to go to the cinema with me the following Saturday.

The date came and went, with little to make it different. She lived with her parents, right in the heart of Ashton, and I walked her home after the movie. Twenty-two-years-old and she had to be back by eleven – this was not a good sign, and the promise was already fading. After the statutory period of smooching, it was actually me who turned to go. It was then that the script took a distinct turn:

'What are you doing Wednesday afternoon?'

I was doing, of course, what I did every Wednesday afternoon in winter – it was our school games afternoon and I would be playing rugby or doing cross country running or something equally exciting. I avoided that as an answer, and thoughtfully answered her question with another one: 'Why?'

'Wednesday's my half day off, and my mam and dad work all day. You can come round here if you want.'

If you want! Oh, I wanted, all right. It just needed some planning, but I would work out the details later. I agreed to come round to her house at two o'clock on the next Wednesday.

The plan, as it emerged, was a jewel of simplicity. I told the sports master I had forgotten my games kit. Such a misdemeanour resulted in a mandatory after-school detention, but the good news is that the penalty occurred on the *Thursday* after school, because the rugby game went on past the normal school ending time on the Wednesday. I was, therefore, unsupervised on the afternoon in question. At half past one I was out of the place like a rat up a drainpipe.

Astonishingly, my memories of what happened next are grainy. They shouldn't be, but they are. Rather surprisingly, they are nothing like as clear and warm and glowing as they are for my first kiss. I do know, however, that when I went through the door of this two-up two-down through-terrace house in Ashton, I manfully played my part in a script, parts of which made *Saturday Night and Sunday Morning* seem like Enid Blyton. She devoured me. For years I had imagined what the mysterious properties of a female genital organ might be – but never, *never*, had I imagined them to be some sort of cross between an industrial vacuum cleaner and an anaconda.

At the time, top athletes were running the two-hundred-yard dash in about twenty two seconds. Today, that has been reduced to about nineteen seconds plus change. In my defence, my deep belief is that my first all-the-way sexual experience lasted for a period of time that was much nearer the former than the latter. The bad news is that the elapsed time, whichever it was, included the fourteen seconds necessary to hood my willy in a condom – a previously untried and therefore clumsy sequence.

Kate seemed remarkably happy with the happenings, and we had a more leisurely repeat after a suitable rest, complete with (and I am *not* making this up) a cup of tea. Somewhere around about three o'clock I was ushered out.

As I lay in my bed late that night, in somewhat reflective mood, two thoughts occurred to me. The first was that the actual act of sex, with a proper woman involved, was OK. But just OK. Frankly, my belief that night was that it couldn't beat the real thing.[4]

My second thought concerned a much more down-to-earth issue. I suddenly realized that my school bag, nestling by my bed, contained a set of rugby kit that was still absolutely clean. A set of circumstances that would be difficult to explain to my parents. I was up and about surprisingly early the next morning. I was the first person downstairs. I nipped outside into the back garden and wiped my rugby kit in a grassy, muddy puddle.

Kate and I repeated all of the above for one more Wednesday. One

---

4 This belief has since changed.

more lie to the sports master, one more deferred detention, one more early escape from school, one more knock on a door at two o' clock, one more devouring, two more shags, one more artificially dirtied rugby kit (this time well in advance) and one more rather disappointed late night reflection.

Two rock-solid certainties did emerge from all this, however. First, Philip Larkin got his timing dead right. Second, in my case, the man-child was no more.

13

The shove that echoed around the world

For Malcolm Taylor, it was 3, 2, 1.

It was the third term in his second year of his first job as a teacher of modern history. The appointment was at our school, and we had just returned after the Easter break. The year was 1964.

Somehow I had reached my school end-game. I was due to take my 'A' levels in a matter of weeks. Malcolm Taylor's History was one of my subjects, the other two being Geography and English Literature. I was a science-free zone. In all three subjects the syllabus was over. The last few weeks were dedicated to revising and trying to draft answers to possible questions.

Mr. Taylor was a tall, fresh-faced, (still) young man, equipped with a full head of somewhat unruly hair, a set of (then fashionable) half-framed spectacles, and the beginnings of a double chin. In the lesson previous to the one that changed my life, he had announced that our homework was to revise the causes of World War One. This regularly came up as a question, so the plan – quite sensibly – was that we would use the next lesson to answer it under exam conditions.

The next lesson arrived. I had actually done as requested and revised the subject, and was reasonably at peace with the world.

And then it all went wrong. Let's face it: my rebel act of the previous handful of years had fallen short of its intended effect. I had not changed the world. In fact, the world had taken sod-all notice. Worse, in some ways, I had survived intact – with endless detentions, innumerable beatings, and selected losses of privileges mere pitfalls en route to taking my 'A' levels with the rest of the upper sixth. I had even had an interview with Coventry University to cover the unlikely occurrence of a stellar performance in the upcoming exams.

In short, an uneasy peace had broken out. My great rebellion had achieved the effect – on the world *and* me – of banging on the window with a sponge. All this changed about thirty seconds after we sat down.

From the front of the class, Malcolm Taylor announced a change of plan. Instead of answering, under exam conditions, the question about the causes of World War One, we would answer a question on Bismarck's foreign policy.

There was silence, and then uproar. Twenty odd seventeen- and eighteen- year-olds who, under the imminent threat of *real* exams, had actually done the homework requested, were suddenly faced with the idea that a) they had just wasted two nights and b) they knew fuck-all about what they were now expected to write on for forty minutes.

Mr. Taylor was unrepentant and unflinching. He explained that what lay ahead of us was the challenge of taking exams as well as the dealing with the content. We would undoubtedly be unpleasantly surprised at some stage during the upcoming weeks. We would undoubtedly be faced with a question that had not, and could not have, been planned in advance. Part of our ability to succeed would be how we reacted in those circumstances, and that was what we were now going to test. There was a gradual resigned silence from everybody – apart from one. That would be me.

From my strategic position at the back of the class, I let fly. I can't remember the exact words, but it was a powerful piece of oratory, running along the lines that I had better things to do with my full, value-adding, life than waste two nights on something that was then useless and blah blah blah…

The speech didn't go down to well with Mr Taylor. His face reddened, and he just snapped. I was told to leave the classroom and wait outside for him. He would deal with me later. I got up from my desk and made my way down the aisle. As I got to the front, I passed Malcolm Taylor very closely. Too closely, as it happens.

He was glaring at me angrily as I walked towards him. I glared back – and as I passed him I gave him a shove. I say 'shove' – I 'sort of' pushed him as he was 'sort of' in my way. No big deal.

Er… oh, yes, it was. As shoves go, it was a game-changer. He dropped and stopped everything else and marched me to Exeley's office, where I was told to stand outside while he went in to give his version of events. As I remember, I was never asked mine. I began to realise something different was happening.

I was eighteen by then. Caning had stopped (my theory being that it stopped when we got as big as them). I was summoned in to Exeley and given a calm quiet direction: to leave the school, go home and await developments.

When I got home about mid-afternoon (I didn't rush) my father, to my surprise, was already there. Again, there was no eruption, no bouncing off the walls. The school had phoned him, the message was simple and somewhat chilling. I was not to return to school. The syllabus was finished, and they would allow me to take the exams – but other than for the actual taking of the exams I would not be allowed on the premises again. The sting was in the tail: I would not be given any reference by the school – pretty much putting paid to any hope of a university place or decent job no matter how well I did in the exams.

It's worth pausing for thought here, particularly if you are a would-be rebel. To quote the late Patrick Campbell: 'Let's marshal the facts'. My five years of rebellion had been like pissing into a Force Ten headwind. When I raised my game (a.k.a. a 'shove'), what happened? The establishment swatted me like an irritating mosquito, that's what happened. As far as they were concerned, I was left as a tiny bloody smudge on the window. Job done.

It took a while to sink in. My grandfather enthusiastically poured fuel on the flames with several 'I told you so' phone calls to my father. He and I considered our hands, and figured out how we were going to play our cards over the next phase. A lot of long, thoughtful silences occurred, and at the end of one of those I do remember him coming out with the immortal comment: 'What is it with you? Why do you go through life pushing doors marked pull?'

What came next was strange. In World War One, during one of the periods in the trenches where the Germans and the Allies were wiping out thousands of each other before coffee, a Christmas-related unofficial truce occurred. An impromptu game of football took place between the warring sides in no man's land. For the record, the Germans won on penalties. Something similar happened in our house. At a time when, all things considered, hostilities should have been escalating – they cooled.

All parties realised that, with the 'A' levels a couple of weeks off, the only way to *start* to salvage anything from this mess was to for me to pass them.

So I did. The record books show nothing special in terms of grades but, given the circumstances, it was a big deal for all concerned. Kirk and Barratt also got theirs and took 'A'-level-entry jobs, while Sam (who also got his) predictably – but still remarkably – signed as a professional footballer for Sheffield Wednesday. None of our immediate group got to university, but a fairly close friend, David Crompton, whom I played football with at Clayton, went to Liverpool University to read maths. He figures later.

School ended, therefore, for all of us – albeit a few weeks early for me. So, I signed on as a general labourer for Whitbreads again, but this time with a difference. I didn't sign on for a finite summer period as part of their holiday relief programme, I just signed on. I was eighteen, getting quite big and strong, I knew the people and the work, and they were looking for full-time labourers.

Of course, in the eyes of my father, this was a disaster right up there with the fall of Singapore. Surely, this could was only be an interim, transitional game-plan. I had 'A' Levels and somewhere, somehow, there was a suitable 'proper', white-collar job or profession that would or could rise above my lack of references and re-establish me on the journey to a respectable middle-class career. I was not so sure or, indeed, enthusiastic, about that idea. My base pay was about £17.00 a week with guaranteed extra from overtime (which was a weird result of 1960s trades' union power). I had five free pints of beer a day. I had no responsibilities. Arthur Seaton, here I come.

Dave Ewing had played for my beloved Manchester City in the late 1950s, in front of my hero Bert Trautmann. He could be described, politely, as an old-school centre half. His preferred direction for kicking the ball was the one in which he was facing. His speciality was heading – a skill he perfected, even while lying down. I am convinced that, had he been available and at his peak in 1944, if we had landed him in Normandy ahead of Private Ryan and his brothers, it would have all been over in weeks. Albeit with a few more casualties. He was now on his way down the leagues, as player-manager of the local semi-professional team Ashton United, whose home ground was half way between our house and the Whitbread depot where I worked. With David Crompton ('Crummer') having left for Liverpool, when the new football season started there was no point in carrying on playing for Clayton, who were based about ten miles and two bus rides away, so I looked for a new team. A local guy I knew invited me to come along to Ashton United to train with them to see if I could raise my game to semi-pro level.

I was reasonably fit. The manual part of my labouring job was physically demanding. I had never smoked. My eating and drinking habits (swollen by my five pints a day from Whitbread) saw my frame filling out – and the needle on the bathroom scales soon enthusiastically passed thirteen stone on its (almost) lifelong clockwise journey. So I went for a trial.

I trained twice with Dave Ewing and his squad. I got two games with their reserve team, but it was not to be. I was just not good enough for that level, but I went on to splash about in the shallow end of the amateur game for years to come.

The short association with Ashton United did, however, produce another result. Right by the ground was a 'mom and pop' sweets and tobacco shop. 'Pop' was a guy called Cliff Rawlinson, who had a day job working as an administrative assistant for Shell-Mex and BP in Manchester. The proper name for the job was 'clerk'. Cliff was a sallow, skinny guy. His hair, greying and greased back, was already showing the yellowish tinge I was beginning, even then, to associate with a lifetime of heavy smoking. But he was friendly, chatty and thoughtful, and I used to banter with him cheerfully as I bought my frequent Wagon Wheel.

After one of my Ashton training sessions he told me that his company had a vacancy for another clerk – sorry, Administrative Assistant – and he thought I'd be a good fit for it. He could get me an interview during the following week. Would I be up for it?

It rocked me on my heels a bit. Things were drifting downhill at home. If I stick with the historic analogies, the impromptu World War One truce had drifted into an atmosphere not unlike that between Russia and Great Britain before the first Afghan invasion of 1839 – a period known as the 'Great Game' when the air was riddled with mistrust and deceit. I had recently opened a letter, addressed to me, that began: 'Dear Mr Gibbons, further to your request to join the army...' That was one of my father's more subtle moves.

Nothing ventured, nothing gained. I bought a suit. I went for the interview primarily to gain some brownie points with the my father. Cliff picked me up one morning at 8.15 and drove me into the offices of Shell-Mex and BP on Oxford Road, Manchester. This nice, helpful man provided something that the united powers of the establishment had dramatically removed some months earlier – i.e. some sort of reference – and I was offered the job.

My father thought he and I had (jointly) won the Pools. I was to work for a company that had Shell in its name, which was right up there with the civil service – and which put me right back on a career track and gave him some sort of bragging rights as to my respectability. All problems solved.

I was not so sure. The 'salary' (note: it was no longer a wage) was about half of what I had been earning. I had to wear a suit, collar and tie and it was a car journey into and out of Manchester every day. The car was Cliff's, and I shared the petrol money with him. It is only after the passing of many years, and an increasingly cynical outlook on life, that I now sometimes reflect that his motives on getting me the job might have been more to do with reducing his fuel bill than getting me back on the straight and narrow.

And, man, was it boring. So the W Gene kicked in again. The company obviously thought I was 'development material', so they gave me a day off each week to attend the Manchester College of Commerce where I would study for a Higher National Diploma (HND) in Business Studies. I decided this was just too good to miss, so simply played truant on about fifty per cent of my college days – gaining myself a free day in Manchester every other week or so. What could possibly go wrong? Here we go again…

Back at the house, the Great Game was drifting into the Cold War. I stuck it for a few months, and then saw an opportunity to change everything. Shell-Mex and BP had a small regional office in Liverpool, with a few positions similar to the one I had in Manchester. On the grapevine, I heard a vacancy had cropped up. I applied for it. I got it.

David Crompton – now nearing the end of his first year at Liverpool University – shared a flat with three other students. The whole thing was something of a health risk, but his room had a spare bed.

I took up the offers of both job and bed.

14

You'll never walk alone

By the mid 1960s Liverpool was, possibly, the coolest place on earth. Never mind the ageing tenements, the high unemployment, the horrendous re-housing tower blocks and the crumbling docks: it had the Beatles. The four strong line-up of drums/base/rhythm and lead guitar, some powerful amplifiers, a bunch of homemade songs, four irreverent cheeky-chappie characters and a marketing genius as a manager all combined to create something *way* in excess of the sum of its parts to capture the zeitgeist of the Boomer's planet. As a by-product, by my count, the city also contained about five thousand me-too groups. I didn't choose to go to Liverpool for any of this. I went to Liverpool to get out of Manchester – or, more particularly, to a house about ten miles east of it.

The job was the same, albeit in a smaller area office. All around me at Shell-Mex House in Manchester were surprised by my move. The big centre, the centre where a young, aspiring administrative assistant might get noticed, was Manchester. That was not what I was, or what I wanted.

The flat I moved into was astonishingly fit for purpose, although our definition of 'purpose' surely differed profoundly from the landlord's. It was the whole of the upper floor, plus a third converted attic floor, of a big detached house in Penny Lane – a handful of miles south of the city centre and university campus, and later to be immortalised by the Fab Four. It had three bedrooms on the main floor (one of them a double-sized room with twin beds), and a single room in the attic. The main floor also had a common room and a large separate kitchen. The

The Liverpool Likely Lads: Chris Monahan on the left, the author in the centre, Dave Crompton front right and Peter Brewer at the back.

place, the people and the script blended the various TV series – the *Likely Lads*, a male-only version of *Friends*, *Men Behaving Badly* and, less likely, *Steptoe and Son* (reflecting the state we kept it in).

Leader of the tribe was Chris Monahan. He and two of the other three were doing doctorates in some advanced science. I took a big liking to Chris, who was phlegmatic in the extreme with a healthy touch of Dr Spock's logic. He was still recovering from being hit by a car while on a motor scooter, an accident which broke and battered him severely – but he had recovered well enough to continue as a very capable amateur athlete. If you caught sight of him from the right direction, in the right light, his body seemed to be made up entirely of right angles.

Man, could he sleep. Twelve hours was a cat nap; twenty-four hours out-for-the-count was about par – and he once, famously, slept through his electric blanket catching fire. He was saved (as were we all) by the rest of us noticing smoke coming from under his door.

Away from home, and away from home cooking, my diet suffered. Although I had lost my five pints a day free beer allowance, it was still the working man's drink and priced accordingly – so my consumption stayed hovering around the 'extremely unhealthy' mark on the dial.

Added to that was my diet of seriously crap food and the needle on the bathroom scales picked up speed on its clockwise mission and whistled past the fourteen stone mark.

My social life now overlapped heavily with student life. I lived with students, and knew nobody else in the city. Crummer could get me into the Student's Union bars, dances and concerts – and those provided pretty much everything I needed (or could afford) on the social front.

Someone else had made the move from Manchester to Merseyside. One of the girls who was loosely in our group back in Manchester had moved to Birkenhead, just the other side of the River Mersey from Liverpool. We first came across her through Geoff Barratt who, at one of our parties back in Denton, had managed to get her upstairs when the lights dimmed. He had been hoping for a heavy necking session, possibly with some 'Upstairs Outside'. At the post-match conference where he was interviewed by about six of us, he came out with the legend-making words: 'You're not going to believe this, but just as I was combing my hair, *she grabbed my knackers.*' I can remember what happened next with the accuracy of a timed video. A pause occurred of exactly four seconds while we all considered this statement and then six voices, in unison and with a harmony that would have made the Everly Brothers proud, chorused: 'You were doing *WHAT?*'

Let's face it, everybody who lived in the 1960s exaggerates the sexual freedoms that are supposed to have pervaded every one's lives, but in fairness this lass – let's just call her Margaret – would have been a solid candidate for stoning to death under Sharia law at any time during the last thirteen hundred years.

Back to Liverpool. Crummer had twigged that she had moved, and they had a few dates together – then he waltzed into the flat one day and announced it was over. At least two of the audience hadn't been aware it had started, but I had, and I could tell he was down. In the words of Wodehouse, it was not difficult to differentiate between him and a ray of sunshine. Ever ready to help a friend, I suggested we went out together on the upcoming Saturday. The Rockin' Berries (I'm serious, for Christ's sake) were playing the Union. It sounded promising for a few pints, a few dances and who knew?

Cometh the hour, we set off to carry out Plan A. We were a (good) few pints through Phase 1 (the drinking), and had left ourselves a bit tight for time for Phase 2 (the dancing). With only a few dances left, I spotted two girls dancing together. One was a petite brunette, the other a bit taller and fairer. I quite fancied the brunette, but I wanted to give Crummer first choice as he was still on the rebound from the loss of Margaret, and as the evening wore on, and he shifted more Higsons Ales, his face took on more of the texture of a slapped arse. I gambled by giving him first choice, knowing he would choose the blonde as she looked vaguely like Margaret. And I do mean vaguely. In all fairness, it wasn't really a gamble. He headed for the fair-haired girl in a vaguely straight line.

BINGO.

Isn't it great when a plan comes off?

After the last two or three dances, the lights went up. I'd put a bit of a shift in, so I thought I'd have a go at getting a phone number from the petite brunette. I'd found out she was a teacher, from Wales, and when she retrieved her coat, it was leather. A teacher, from Wales, with a *leather coat*. Jesus. Clearly this was a class act, and worth pursuing. I think, in the end, she gave me her phone number to get rid of me. They were cleaning the dance floor before she gave in though.

I mentioned this to Monahan the next day. He scoffed. There was no way, he scoffed on, that I could go out with a teacher, from Wales, particularly one with a leather coat, for – let's say – a month. And he promptly bet me five pounds that it couldn't be done. Confucius, he say 'life for men is a dick-measuring contest' and I wasn't having this sleight to my ability to punch above my weight for a month. The bet was taken.

To my surprise and delight (five pounds was a lot of money in 1965), she – her name was Judy – agreed to my romantic proposal to come and see *The Battle of the Bulge* at the cinema, and then topped everything by agreeing to come out again on a date which (through careful planning) would have carried me beyond the month. Monahan never paid up.

Meanwhile, on another front, the W Gene was getting restless. I had escaped from Manchester without taking the HND exams, so Shell-Mex promptly failed to notice the signs and enrolled me in the same course at Liverpool College of Commerce. That gave me a similar day off a week to attend lectures. And, wouldn't you know, I spat this act of generosity right back in their face by starting to take frequent college days off.

The HND course was run by a guy from Liverpool University doing a bit of moonlighting. His name was Professor Nelson. One day, on one of my rare attendances, he asked me to stay behind after class. This was not good news. In my life, nothing good had ever come from such a summons, and my performance and behaviours indicated I was about to re-enter choppy waters, probably with a head wind. You could have got long odds against correctly forecasting what followed.

One to one, he just looked at me. There was a long pregnant silence, reminiscent of those that had occurred frequently between my father and me. Then it came. 'Why are you behaving like this? In my opinion, you should be up here lecturing to the class and not fooling about with your career and life.' There followed a pregnant pause, before he quietly carried on. 'Let me tell you what I can do. IF [my capitals] you pass the HND this summer, I will get you into Liverpool University, to read for an honours degree in Business Studies as a full-time mature student in October. Let me know next week.'

Wow. The W Gene went all quiet. Even I recognised that this was a potential game changer. It was a long bus ride back to the flat – with my thought processes strangely concentrating not on the implications of taking up his offer, but the implications of not so doing.

While all this was going on, Judy and I had drifted past the thirty-day mark, and then drifted past another one. Then another one. In fact, to use a cricketing analogy, we were both beginning to be of the view that we had seen the shine off the new ball, and could be in for a long knock together. So I told her my news. The implications were (in no particular order): I would, first, have to get the HND; I would have to leave Shell; I would have to get a local authority grant and find some way of working through university to make up the monetary shortfall. And I would have to break the news to my father who would undoubtedly see leaving Shell as sliding down a snake after climbing a few ladders. I had no track record of pulling off anything like this.

What to do? I looked at Judy for some sort of signal.

To this day I cannot remember what she said. But to this day I haven't forgotten the look she gave me.

Book Two

Lord of the files

*If you want to make God really laugh, show him
your business plan.*

Anon

15

Send her victorious

Why on earth would the invitation be in *French*? It wasn't as though it was hard to translate – I mean, most of us could scramble through VENDREDI LE 17 MAI 1991 and figure the actual day out. But would a similar missive, issued from the upper slopes of the French societal pyramid, be in English? I think not, and it put me on the wrong foot from the get-go. This was, after all, an invitation to dine, quite intimately, on board a boat, a very big boat, with my Queen.

The instructions had been ever-so specific. Our limo (there was no nonsense here – it was assumed you would arrive in a Stretch) was to arrive, at the dockside, between 6.55 and 7.10 p.m. For all the world it sounded like one of the day-plans worked out by my secretary – which were then typed up on 6 by 3-inch cards and given to me with a bundle of air tickets at the start of every trip. ('Tuesday, 6.30 a.m. – get up, crap, clean your teeth, shave, dress, leave hotel room, turn right, take elevator down twenty floors, go in the breakfast bar, meet Mr. Ushida, bow slightly, repeat slightly, remark how nice new Tokyo airport is, don't mention the war, ask after his father who is something big in the Kirin Brewing company … maybe mention his daughter Sukiyaki who has been ill with chickenpox recently…)

Working on the basis that you don't mess around with a head of state, we left in good time, knowing the downtown Miami traffic was, at best, unpredictable in the early evening. The city's automobile population was peppered with huge Lincoln town cars that meandered at low speeds over critical intersections, seemingly without drivers. It was only on closer inspection that you spotted two tiny liver-spotted hands on the steering wheel and a wisp of blueish hair protruding above the seat back. It would be, indeed, some semi-embalmed tiny widow, aged around one hundred, plus or minus a couple of standard deviations, driving her recently departed husband's gas-guzzler to a set of highway rules known only to herself but which could, and did, grind the city to a halt. If the indicator light was flashing, it had probably been so doing when she first got the car.

I had grown to hate limos. They had come to represent the opposite of everything I was trying to be and do – but tonight all that was defenestrated.[5] The two of us sprawled in the dark mini-cavern that was the back part of one of the longest you have ever seen. We were just about within shouting distance of the driver. Judy looked like a bobbie-dazzler; for once, she had entered into the spirit of the world of south Florida's female glitterati and had spent the equivalent of a small Asian country's GDP on an outfit.

To be honest, so had I. I had a feeling that my Marks and Spencer's dinner suit (or my 'tux' as it was known in the US) wouldn't stand up to an evening like this, particularly as the pants had a rather embarrassing stain down the front. If my memory served me, this stain had something to do with oysters.[6] Anyway, I was now the proud possessor of an Armani tux, costing north of $1000, which (for those of you interested in this kind of thing) remains with me to this day and which is running in at a sunk cost of about $333 per outing so far.

Eventually, the Stretch pulled in by the dockside at a clearly defined spot where passengers were required to disembark. From the inside we could see out, and our eyes and minds digested the crowd of photographers and newspaper hacks awaiting to see what or who our limo coughed up. From outside, of course, courtesy of darkened windows, you couldn't see in – so that none of the media hounds could get an anticipatory glance and register the fact that nobody they had ever heard of inhabited this particular vehicle. When we got out, blinking in south Florida's hard evening sunset glare, the waves of apathy were almost audible. No Stallone in this one, then. No matter. We smiled at each other for reassurance, and disappeared inside the door of this enormous tent.

5 Thrown out the window.
6 Honest...

I don't know what I had been expecting, but it wasn't the sight that met us. Quite serious – and I mean *serious* – armed troops greeted us. When I say greeted, it wasn't the sort of greeting you got in your local bar, it was the kind of greeting you might give to some chewing gum that had become attached to the sole of your shoe. This was a security check, and it was not one of those perfunctory ones you got at the airport prior to 9/11. Oh, no; this was a *security check*, and the guys doing it were never solo, and wore black uniforms and had blacked-up faces. Each was armed with enough weaponry (it seemed to me) to kit out six Rambo films. Smiles were at a premium.

Eventually, they decided that Judy's dainty purse was unlikely to contain a heat-seeking missile, let us through and we emerged through the back door of the tent into the light again. We were right next to the stairs by which you boarded the ship. I say 'ship' because this vessel was commonly called a yacht, but from where I was – at the bottom of the boarding stairs looking up – this was a ship and a big bastard at that. We climbed aboard, promptly to be submerged in a sea of attendants offering us cocktails. Judy gave me a look that I know well. She doesn't give it me often, so when she does she means it. It's a look that says 'don't get pissed'.

The next bit is little fuzzy in my memory. I remember eating canapés as though they were plankton, which is a weakness of mine when I'm nervous. Then there's a hazy bit and then we were suddenly in a line – and I was talking to the Duke of Edinburgh. I can't remember what we talked about for our regulation eighteen seconds, and I'm sure if you were to ask him he would be equally vague. In my case there was a good reason for being disinterested. Two paces behind him, and already in my line of sight (despite the fact I was staring fixedly to the front at Phillip's wrinkles) was my Sovereign. As it happens she went past me like Road Runner, and without much further ado we were ushered in for dinner aboard the Royal Yacht Britannia.

The three dining tables were in a 'U' shape, with the top table consisting of the President of the United States and his stick-insect of a wife – Ronnie and Nancy Reagan. Correction, they would have both been there, but he was under the weather,[7] so it was just Nancy. Another (ex) President, Gerald Ford, and his wife Betty – she of the Clinic – were also at the top table. Liz and Phil made up the top table numbers – along

---

7   This may have been caused by his black hair dye coming out too orangey.

with Douglas Hurd, a British Cabinet minister, and the Bishop of Miami. This squad looked down on the other two tables.

Judy and I were split – facing each other on either side of the 'U'. Next to me was a lady who had her finger in every pie to do with the 'arts' in Miami. This woman could bore for America should they ever include it in the Olympics – and that, in my observation, would be a very difficult team to get into; trust me, there would be fierce competition. I have no memory of who was on my left, and I suspect I left much the same impression on him or her.

Facing me, and generally hampering my ability to see anything ahead, was a vase, with an extensive array of flowers pointing up and hanging over its edges. It seemed to be the size of a small Dodge pick-up truck. While I was eating my starter, I managed to read the inscription on the side, and it gradually sank in that this vase, a gift from some oil-rich sheikdom, was *made of gold*. J-e-s-u-s. I can't remember the exact figure, but that afternoon my desktop screen had been indicating that the price of gold was a trifle anti-gravitational on account of the recession we were experiencing at the time. I think it was pushing $400 an ounce, and I immediately began calculating how much this monstrosity right in front of my nose was worth. That's the vase, not the arts lady.

By the time I had given up, I had eaten my starter and not noticed the contents. Looking at the menu, it appeared that I had partaken of something or of some things called 'Oeufs Drumkilbo'. To this day I have no idea what they are, but I have asked for them ceaselessly in restaurants of repute around the world. Result? Not a sniff, not a sniff. I will keep looking.

We then made our way through a simple but gorgeously cooked and presented meal – again, all listed on the menu card in stupendously annoying French. I don't have a problem with pretension, acknowledging the research that recorded that ninety per cent of the purchases that men make are done for the impact they will have on other people. The only quarrel I have with it is that, on reflecting my own experience, it's about nine points south of the truth. But some ultra-pretentious things do annoy me. Why the Queen of England should play along with such foreign bollock-speak is beyond me.

The fun really began after dinner, when we adjourned to an anteroom and were joined by a much bigger group of guests for coffee and liqueurs. The dinner party had involved no more than twenty or twenty-five invited guests, whereas the next bit opened the event up to about a hundred of Miami's (sort of) B-plus-list celebrities. In that Never Never Land of bad taste and bullshit, where status wasn't next to Godliness, it *was* Godliness, to be invited to the dinner gave life-long bragging rights. To be invited to the second part of the evening gave lifelong bragging rights against people who had not been invited at all, but a serious inferiority positioning against those who hit the lottery win of dinner with the Queen. True to form, having made the A List, I was an absolute prick. And here it comes, the first appearance of the W Gene in Book Two. I spent ten minutes with Dante Fascell, south Florida's long serving and highly respected Congressman, talking about the Oeufs Drumkilbo he'd missed out on.

The astute among you will be questioning how I got our top-twenty royal dinner positioning in a city some 4500 miles away from my birth. The simple fact is that I had recently been appointed Chairman and CEO of one of the world's biggest branded businesses. The world headquarters of Burger King Corporation, at that time trading in more than 40 countries and with about 7000 restaurants, was in Miami. The company I had been working for in England, GrandMet, had acquired a large US conglomerate called Pillsbury[8] in one of the last big contested acquisitions of the 1980s. They had seen fit to send me over to run it – and to live there, together with my wife, one of our two sons, and a pedigree Golden Retriever. Fairly shortly after our arrival, the son who had accompanied us indicated how impressed he was with teenage Miami by choosing to go back to England to board at his old school with his brother. We compensated by flying out a second Golden Retriever puppy. My mission was to breathe life into Burger King Corporation, which had found itself in a life-threatened situation after some years of neglect.

More of that in a bit, but for now all you need to digest is that an invitation had been issued, via the British Consul, to a handful of British business people in the port of Miami – Britannia's only US stop on this particular tour of the Third and Fourth Worlds. Of course, when the invitation dropped through my corporate letterbox, all hell let loose back at GrandMet's UK headquarters. I mean, there were several potential knighthoods ahead of mine in the queue, and there was immediate pressure to bump me and get a proper GrandMet Statesman exposed to Her Maj.

---

8   The Pillsbury Group included the Pillsbury, Green Giant, Häagen-Dazs and Burger King brands.

In all honesty, I wasn't bothered. Rather strangely, in my short time in Miami, I had already been exposed to the delights of an intimate royal visit – when Prince Michael of Kent decided to visit me in my new outpost of British corporate exploration. I say 'decided' when, in reality, I have no idea of the machinations behind the visit, but I do know that in style, goals and outcome it bore no relation to the later Sovereign's pop-in. Bonnie Prince Michael's visit involved the writing of a large $US cheque and the loan of our private plane. Allen Sheppard, the head of GrandMet and my ultimate boss, was knighted not long after this visit, and lorded not long after that. I have no real idea if these circumstances represented some degree of cause and effect, but I hope so. I don't know why else I had to put up with the bearded one.

Prince Michael did not arrive in the best of circumstances. Burger King was an iconic American company, run mostly by US franchisees – the bulk of whom could be politely described as corporate rednecks. To this gaggle, which I suspect to be the collective noun for such businessmen, the taking over of BK by a British company, with the addition of a (relatively) young English Chairman/CEO who confessed to knowing FA about the business made for some mildly strained early relationships. Luckily, they soon got worse.

Back to Beardy. When the detailed pre-visit protocol instructions arrived, I nearly had a fit. It was something I thought the Magna Carta should have addressed. I was faced with calling a bunch of my staff in on a Saturday, and – for those lucky to get such a call – instructing them in the art of bowing, curtseying, and how to 'behave' in royalty's presence. It was left to Ron Petty, my most senior inherited American executive, to calm my fears. Ron was a Texan who measured about 5' 8" up and down and side to side, and as fiercely American as they come – but he told me not to worry. Everybody, he said with a grin as wide as his head, would love all the weird ritual.

And so they did. When Prince Michael eventually arrived – suitably late on a Saturday afternoon – everybody went over the top. I was silent for the early part of his visit, my mind being completely taken up by his tie knot. How the hell do you get a tie knot the size of Fatty Arbuckle's coffin? To this day I don't know. In fairness, it helped that we all recognised that he wasn't from our planet; he arrived in Miami wearing a woollen suit and never sweated a single drop. All my folk were wonderful, although, to be fair, some of them got the instructions mixed up a bit. I had guys curtseying, I had women bowing. Some addressed him as the King, and I think one guy invented 'Your Godship'. One guy, a lifetime non-smoker, got the very detailed instructions on smoking protocol in his presence all wrong – and lit up.

We eventually got him out of his Bentley (produced from I know not where) up to the research kitchen, where the plan was to ignore the clear instructions that royalty must *never* be photographed eating and to get one of Him holding a Whopper (hamburger). It was here that he spoke some of his few words on the day. Peering at a burger starting its journey into the mini crematorium that cooks it, he turned to me and uttered the immortal words 'Hoy miny do you get oyt of a coy?'

I stared back blankly. I had no idea of what he spake or in what language he had spake it.

He repeated 'How miny do you get *oyt of a coy*?'

The last bit was up a decibel or so, as if that would clarify it all. It did. Frantically working it out in my own mental Enigma decoder, I realised he was asking how many hamburger patties we got out of a cow. The bad news? I had absolutely no fucking idea. Not even a clue. I turned to Ron, a lifetime burger man, and asked him. He had come prepared to answer *anything* on or about Burger King, or the wider hamburger industry. Anything, that is, apart from this. It went down a short line of white-coats who were standing by as back-up. No answer came back up the line. I turned to the Bearded One and answered. 'About 2900 on average, sir.'

As we found out later the correct answer to the question 'How many burger patties do Burger King get out of a steer?' is, of course, that we started in 1956, and we haven't used the first one up yet. That's a big hamburger industry joke. Honest.

Prince Michael eventually boarded his Bentley and left. At the time, it had been my first experience of British royalty – albeit a rather peripheral member of this evolutionary cul-de-sac – in my forty-four years on the planet. I had no idea that the Big One – the Real Thing – was just around the time corner.

Back to dinner on Britannia, and my response as the 'invitation' landed on my desk .

Even after Michael's rather off-putting visit, like many or most of the UK population I had no great feelings either way for the royal family. Since then, with all that Diana bollocks and the endless pratting about of Elizabeth's assorted offspring and relatives, my position on the subject has drifted towards that of Robespierre. But right there, right then, I was not bothered either way. In truth, I didn't really fancy all the hoopla that would be involved in such an event – and would have quite happily given up my seat just below the salt – when the local British Consul played a joker and pissed them all off back at the corporate ranch. A follow-up edict arrived, which they said was from the Palace, to the effect that the invitation was only to British businesspeople who were *actually in place* at the port of call. Once I knew that, I was like a pit bull. Nobody was nicking my invite. Knighthood-schmighthood.

The evening progressed. At 11.00 p.m. promptly we were summoned outside, interrupting a balls-aching conversation I was having with Douglas Hurd about a novel he was writing or had just written. In fairness, it was balls-aching for him as well; I had nothing of interest for him which might have ratcheted the chat's excitement up a notch. Ambling out on to the deck, one of those gorgeous Miami nights was suddenly made many degrees warmer as the Queen's band struck up – while they were marching up and down the quayside in their white uniforms. This was the stuff that got your blood rushing. It was no wonder we conquered the Indian subcontinent with about twenty troops; if they were backed up with military bands like this I'm surprised anybody could have resisted us. There was a handsome crowd from the City pressed against the railings watching the march past, and the bandsmen's eyes only wondered from the front to line up a bit of Latino tottie for later on. There was plenty to choose from.

The Queen waved to the band and the people and the stars. Then it was all over. We went home, with the limo picking us up within two minutes of the pre-scheduled departure time. I still had the rousing military music in my ears as we flopped in the back and set off to the 6000-square-feet mansion-cum-hangar that was our US home. I made myself a promise.

A number of my Board of Directors, and indeed, many less eminent employees of Burger King, had boats, this being Florida and the sea and beaches being a way of life. Some of those boats were called yachts – and deservedly so. They were big, stylish vessels. I had neither boat nor yacht and no desire for either. I had put this down to a piece of received wisdom – that if you want to float it or fly it you should rent it, not own it. After this event, however, I immediately realised that my subconscious held another inhibitor. That night I decided that I would never own a yacht unless it was big enough to house a military band, and of such stature that I didn't know they were actually travelling with me when we went to sea. Now *that's* a yacht.

I'm not there yet.

During the evening I had obeyed the spirit of Judy's well-meant directive, limiting myself to a glass or two of wine and some sort of after dinner liqueur. The effects of a long day, however, began to catch up and I felt myself dozing in the back of the limo. Limos, royal yachts, glitterati, tuxedos, CEO-ships et al. all started to blur and gradually got mixed up with other images. Tomorrow would be another day, with the tinselly stuff discarded and the promise of a lonely spell in my (deliberately) sparse office. I had a gap of approaching $200 million between the company's current level of projected earnings and where the City analysts (and my bosses) expected us to be. That's a $200 million shortfall, in case you were wondering. I needed a plan.

16

Where was that again?

Before the plan, let's press the rewind button and go back nearly three years. It is the summer of 1988. It's a big jump from the end of Book One, so I'll scatter few clues as to what I've become and what's happened to me. Here's the first: I am driving a Range Rover the size of a small village shop. I have not acquired the Wellingtons with buckles on, but it is clear I am well on the way to being something and someone I previously despised.

Here's a second one: we are still living in England, but I am driving to catch the car ferry to France for a private holiday. At the last moment, I had been summoned to call in and see Allen Sheppard, the Chairman and Chief Executive of the company I work for, Grand Metropolitan (GrandMet). It was, apparently, the only possible time we could meet to discuss this confidential topic without me cancelling the holiday. Now then: another clue. In a previous life, that would have signalled imminent trouble and a teaspoonful of soul-searching on my behalf as I mentally trawled through the potential trouble I'd been in or caused. Not now.

The biggest problem I was currently facing was to get a business card wide enough to contain my current corporate title – which was Chairman and Chief Executive of the Berni and Host Group Ltd., a wholly owned subsidiary of the aforementioned GrandMet. This is not a business book, but you need some idea of where that company had been and what it was (and what, therefore I was) currently doing if you are going to be able to put what comes next into some sort of context. Here goes:

- GrandMet flourished after the World War Two on the back of a person and a very solid idea. The person was Maxwell Joseph, and the idea was that you couldn't go far wrong in investing in property-based businesses. He started with Grand Metropolitan hotels.

- Another opportunity soon appeared on his radar. The UK brewing industry had grown over hundreds of years into a massive property-owning sector. Over those years, the breweries had increasingly bought pubs, rented them to operators and then 'tied' them as outlets for their beer brands and other controlled-supply products. For decades this was a formula for getting rich without getting out of bed. That's the kind of formula that attracts predators, and the industry began a post-war consolidation.

- This formula ticked all the boxes for Maxwell Joseph and his successor Stanley Grinstead, and GrandMet began acquiring. The brands and pub portfolios of Watneys, Manns, Trumans, Wilsons (etc., etc.) were acquired, and GrandMet ended up owning five or six thousand pubs, a bunch of breweries and a load of drinks brands. They then added a property-based restaurant chain (Berni Inns) for good measure. The same principles applied.

- If you want to make God really laugh, show him your business plan. It's the quote I opened this Book with, and it's an old adage, but it's also a gem – just when you think you've got it all sorted, something happens to threaten the best of plans. As the 1970s passed, a number of clouds appeared and began raining on this parade. Beer sales tailed off as drink-drive legislation started to bite; beer duty pushed the heavy-volume-drinking price out of the range of the working man; a trend for less volume but more alcohol got some traction and our entry into Europe via the Treaty of Rome threatened the traditional 'tie' which was the glue that held the whole thing together for the property-owning brewers.

- As sales volumes stalled it became harder to get returns, so guess what? The properties stopped being maintained properly. The wholesale margins were pushed up. Rents were pushed up. Amazingly, these added to the declining attraction of the market to its operators and customers, so the cushy returns not only continued to be squeezed, but began to look unsustainable. Something had to be done.

• Anything other than a superficial analysis indicated that evolution was not going to fix this – it needed revolution. And revolution needs a series of revolutionaries – veritable Robespierres, men and women wearing a Big S on their vest fronts and with their underpants worn outside their trousers. Apparently, this is where I came in.

Teams were assembled across the industry to address a five-part strategy:

1. Sell off no-hope pubs.

2. Rely less on drinks income (which was declining) and more on food and gaming machines (which was growing).

3. Completely restructure the tie – with less reliance on tied product profits and more reliance on commercial property rents (which would include full repairing provisions).

4. Bring professionalism into (drinks) brand-owning and wholesaling because both were going to have to compete in untied markets.

5. Cream off the best pubs and restaurants and directly manage them as a wholly-tied retail business.

Number Five is where I came in. We left Book One with me in Liverpool, after I had applied for a job with Shell-Mex and BP at their regional office there. It was to be the last job I actually applied for in my life. The intervening couple of decades had seen me headhunted a couple of times, the last one being from Whitbread into GrandMet, and I cannot carry on without telling you about my first title in this cutting-edge company. I was recruited as a Group Operations Director (North) for their new retail pub and restaurant operation, the Host Group. It was only after I had started, and I began to be referred to by others in the business by the acronym of my job title, that I realised what I had become, Yup, I was GOD (North). You could spend a week trying, but you couldn't fucking make that up.

Within a year I was a sort of full GOD (aka Chairman and CEO), running about 1500 directly managed pubs and restaurants, mostly in the UK but with some in Europe. We were investing millions to address years of basic maintenance starvation in the fabric of the properties, but also trying to bring the food and drink retail offering into some kind of alignment with what (we perceived) the late-twentieth-century cus-tomer wanted. Some of our early attempts were embarrassing, but there were signs that we were beginning to get the balance right.

It would be safe to say that none of the above was in my mind as I pulled into a parking spot at GrandMet's London Headquarters on that July day in 1988. My biggest concern was that Allen Sheppard had another delayed birthday present for me – just as I felt I was getting a grip on my current portfolio of responsibilities, he'd whack another one in. The last one of these was Berni Inns, hence the wide business card needs. The current gaggle of brands I had were all the managed pubs (Chef and Brewer), Berni, Weinerwald (Germany), Pastaficio, Old Orleans, City Limits, Food Courts and some others you have also never heard of.

Finally, finally, I was ushered into Allen's office and heard the re-doubtable Brenda shut the door behind me. I loved working for Allen (soon to be Sir Allen Sheppard and soon after that to be Lord Didge-mere). He had his detractors and I suspect he ended up frustrated that, although he got all the recognition possible via titles, he never felt the business community gave his triumphs the recognition they deserved. All I know is that he was inspiring to work for. I guess everybody re-members their relationship with somebody like that differently, but in my case he seemed to build his approach to business around three fun-damentals, i.e.:

1. Only employ people who are capable of hitting you.

2. My door is always open – but don't come in with a problem. Come in with a proposed solution.

3. Look after the short-term profits of the business and then guess what? The long-term profits look after themselves.

It was the last one that clouded his achievements and reputation – principally because he achieved it. The issue was 'how' it was achieved. Sometimes agreed accounting principles got bent a bit. I bent a few for him in my time.

All that was ahead of us as I sat down – facing him across a desk you could, with a bit of fiddling and not much wind, land a Sikorski on. It was obviously going to be something game-changing, and my mind had (I thought) trawled all the possibilities, but if I had sat there for a week –

a year – I would never have come up with the one he did. The message was short and simple. From this moment on, I was sworn to some sort of unofficial secrets act. What he was about to tell me was stock price sensitive. If I told anyone, I would have to immediately kill them. GrandMet had, a few days before, submitted an unwelcome and contested offer to acquire a huge American company, the Pillsbury Group. That Group included (amongst others) the Pillsbury flour and baked products company, the Green Giant canned vegetable business, Häagen Dazs ice cream and the Burger King international fast food business. Should the bid be successful, GrandMet would like me to go and run the last named.

I sat there feeling that I was trying to take a sip of water out of a fire hose. About forty thousand thoughts were going out of my head, and coming back in again. The upcoming job challenge at that moment was irrelevant – that could and would come later. First thoughts were about family: where would Judy's mind be? How would it affect the boys? Parents? House and home? Schools? That lot took up about a second in time, at which point I realised I had been making an assumption – that it would be based in the USA. I thought I'd better confirm this fundamental, so I asked him. His face took on that look which I know well, where you have prepared for a load of questions – but not for the one asked. He scrambled around in his brief case and produced a copy of Pillsbury's last annual report, and thumbed through it with a furrowed brow. At last, after what seemed like half a bloody hour he looked up and beamed. Miami.

I beamed back. I thought it appropriate, given that I was incapable of thinking of anything to say. He hammered two final thoughts into my recently-turned-into-balsa-wood brain, and I was out. Those two thoughts were: a) we had only made a bid – and it would be some time before we would be successful if, if, *if* we were actually to be successful and b) if and when this happened, and I accepted the position, in the planned GrandMet superstructure of management, I would report to a head of USA Operations – and my appointment would have to be ratified by him.

What followed was an interesting holiday. I broke the confidentiality rules within, oh, let's say twenty minutes of leaving his office, and then spent much of the ensuing two weeks in Provence evidencing what later became known as the Tiger Woods 1000-yard stare. To say I was preoccupied wouldn't do it justice.

Some decisions are taken not for the implications of taking them, but for the implications of *not* taking them. If I didn't take this offer, I knew I would spend the rest of my life wondering about what might have been. The process was helped by Judy reprising her trick (I can't remember what she said, but I will remember forever the look she gave me…), and we decided that, if the bid was successful, I would accept the offer.

September arrived, and the call came. Pillsbury's management had been overruled by their stockholders and they had accepted GrandMet's (improved) bid. Game on. I was to fly to the USA and be 'ratified' by my new boss to be, with a view to taking up the position as Chairman and Chief Executive Officer, Burger King Corporation, based in Miami, on completion of the acquisition process – probably around the turn of the year. If you are keeping records, I was forty-two. Now, this is where the fun started.

First, what should make an appearance but my old friend the W Gene. Allen Sheppard had told me the job was mine, but I still had to through this process of being seen or ratified or blessed (delete as applicable) by the head of US Operations. This man had a reputation of being po-faced, very strait-laced, hugely status conscious and having had his sense of humour surgically removed at an early age: in fact, pretty much the polar opposite to yours truly. As I understood it, the decision had been made, so this whole process seemed a) redundant and b) open to the W Gene. The possibility of turning up in jeans and a rugby shirt crossed my mind, but a new element was appearing: the ability to throw a fire-blanket on the W Gene and limit its effect when it threatened to damage my outlook, and to let it loose when it might work in my favour. The jeans and rugby shirt were left at home. I decided against the tattoo.

My new status started to become apparent. Still under a cloak of secrecy, I was booked to fly to New York on Concorde, see my man, and come back by return, with the whole visit disguised as a visit to the dentist or something. I can't remember much about the trip, except I sat next to Frank Bruno, the loveable man-child of a British boxer who was flying out for his latest pasting in the US. When we stood up to leave the plane in New York, his manager, who was seated in the row in front of us, straightened Frank's tie and dusted off his lapels for all the world as though he was a school kid heading off for the first day of a new term. Another fun moment occurred outside, where Tony Curtis – returning to the USA after switching on the Oxford Street Christmas lights – waited with me in the car pick up bit, him gripping a luggage trolley with about six Louis Vuitton over-stuffed cases on it. A sedan arrived for him. A stretch limousine, similar in size to the Concorde I'd just flown in on, arrived for me. I began to enjoy aspects of this new life. The 'interview' came and went. I can't remember what was said or discussed, and I doubt he can. I returned from my 'dental visit' to my job with the long title. The cloak and dagger stuff continued – on pain of some sort of death I was to tell nobody, including friends, colleagues and anyone but my closest family. The W Gene made a mini-appearance, and I treated that direction with the merit it deserved – i.e. little or none. My life and the life of my family were to be turned upside down, and plans had to be shaped, decisions with implications had to be taken, arrangements had to be made and things had to be talked about.

I had absolutely no knowledge of Burger King, a brand that had no presence in the UK after a failed entrance into the market a few years before. I had no knowledge of fast food, i.e. counter service. All I knew was that the brand was in trouble, and it was to be mine – so (IMHO[9]) no knowledge is a great starting point. You have no preconceived ideas. What you do have, of course, is a need to find out stuff fast – so I began an off-stage personal research mission. I was 'helped' by a continuous flow of secret 'stuff' from GrandMet's acquisition agents and consultants. I read and re-read all this bumph, and came to a conclusion that has stayed with me ever since: the major role of corporate consultants is to borrow your watch to tell you the time.

We decided to 'join' our parents, all four of whom were getting on but alive and kicking, when we got them together at Christmas – with me due to start up in position a couple of weeks later. Understandably (I think) Judy's parents took it harder than mine, and they were quite distressed by the idea of me whisking their eldest daughter off and putting nearly five thousand miles between her, and their grandchildren, and them. In the end they got over it, and grew to share the excitement. Judy's dad, an ex-policeman and keen beach fisherman in Pembrokeshire, had a personal lifetime record catch of an eight-pound sea bass. He was finally won over when, a couple of years after this Christmas, he visited us in Miami and we rented a boat and went out for a day. He hooked and landed a forty-five-pound amberjack. Problem solved.

---

9   In My Humble Opinion. In extreme circumstances you can add an F between the H and the O...

My last day in the UK finally arrived. The official plan was that, as nobody knew anything because of the serious secrecy clause I had been honouring (!), I would get my UK management team together on some pretext on the actual day I was to leave, have a little 'farewell' event, and maybe split a bottle of sherry between us. I would make an impromptu speech and then head for the airport. As there were no afternoon flights to Miami, I would get a plane to New York in the afternoon, and then the late night flight down to Florida.

To this day I have no real idea exactly how much GrandMet 'Central' believed this whole secrecy game plan had been kept under wraps. My feeling is that you would have to have had a spell around the dark side of the Moon not to pick up on pretty much every detail. This was evidenced by my quiet, low-key farewell event. If they'd have stumped up for a couple of elephants it could have officially been called a circus. As it was, Emma Thompson, the acclaimed actress, signed something for me. As it was, Emlyn Hughes, ex-footballer and TV 'sleb' signed something for me – and – just as I was leaving for the plane, somebody put on a video. It was only the whole of (my beloved) Manchester City football team, filmed a few days before, in their stadium in Manchester, wishing me 'good luck in Burger King'.

About ten hours and two flights later, I checked into the Marriott Hotel in Coral Gables, Miami. The Eagle had landed.

17
The moon landing

My entry into the Burger King 'World Headquarters' the next day was stage-managed. This was appropriate, in a way, because I was entering a badly-scripted sitcom.

I was due to go in there at 10.30 a.m. My USA boss was to fly down from the Pillsbury headquarters in Minneapolis (in the corporate jet, of course) and pick me up at the hotel at 10.15 (in a stretch limousine, of course) and take me in. He had been to the site a couple of times, and had arranged for the 'top one hundred managers' to be assembled in a big conference room where he would introduce me and I would give some sort of Henry the Fifth, rousing, motivating speech. After that, he would be off and I would be on my own. At that stage, based on so-far-received information, I had only a couple of preconceptions about the place. My first one was that one hundred 'top' managers felt about seventy-five too many. My second one was that it must it must be some kind of building that had a conference room on-site that held one hundred bodies.

All that was ahead of me as I awoke on this January day in 1989, for the first day of the rest of my life. Not surprisingly, I woke early and had time to kill before the 10.15 pick-up. I had found out that there was a Burger King near the hotel, which was also the one nearest to the World Headquarters. It was time for some practical, real-life research as I had still never been in one.

A basic rule of running a retail brand, one that has a lot of outlets, is that the outlet nearest the location that houses the boss is perfect. The

rest might be crap, but *that one* is honed and polished and run to the letter of the Operations Manual. The sight and experience that greeted me
as I walked through the door was, therefore, something of a surprise: the
place was a shit-house. It was on US1, the main Florida–Canada route
that hugs the east coast of the USA. It was on the edge of the campus
of the University of Miami. It was about two miles from the corporate
headquarters in the heavily populated suburbs south of the city of Miami. It was peak breakfast time. Traffic in the drive-thru was thin, and I
found myself dining solo inside. Despite my lack of company, the tables
were dirty and uncleared. The floor looked as though it had been last
cleaned in the Kennedy administration, so I gave a visit to the bathroom
a miss. I ordered something called a 'crossandwich', and could cheerfully
have wrung the grease out of it. My coffee was about two degrees north
of Marmite, but with a slightly more savoury taste and a slightly darker
colour. And I was a happy camper.

My good mood harkened back to my experiences as an amateur
footballer. Over many years I experienced a lot of injuries, ranging from
minor cuts to serious bone fractures and, as many Lancastrians do, I
developed a theory about this particular aspect of life. If I could actually
see the damage (usually a cut and/or blood), I was happy. In that case,
the problem was superficial and could usually be sorted. If it hurt and I
couldn't see anything, well, then I worried. What I saw and experienced
in that shabby Burger King looked superficial. My initial thought, as the
fat dribbled down my chin, was that this could be sorted. As it turned
out, it wasn't a bad first thought.

I've mentioned that my US boss was a not known for his sense of
humour. Over the next few years I found this not to be strictly true;
he had one, but only let it out when very few (and very trusted) people
were looking. I got an early example of this as were turned off US1 and
approached the headquarters. He told me, with the faintest of smiles, to
close my eyes – and not to open them until he said to do so. I obeyed,
joining in the fun.

We were inside the campus, about half a mile in from the front gate but
now with the main building(s) in sight, when he told me to open them.
I'd obviously steeled myself for something out of the ordinary, but my first
sight of the headquarters of my new empire pushed me beyond surprise.

If you'd have asked me that night for a summary of what I saw, I
wouldn't have done it justice. It was not until many years later I saw
something that I could use as an analogy. I was back in the UK, driving

my mother up to Carlisle to see her brother, and we stopped at a big ho-
tel/function-room complex near Preston. They specialised in weddings,
and one was going on while we were there. Oh, my word. I got some idea
of the style of this event as I almost bumped into the bride outside the
reception door as she popped out of the proceedings for a roll-up cigarette. When I say popped out, that phrase is also useful in describing her
relationship with her wedding dress. I think, technically, there was more
of her out of it than in it – but that's not what really caught my eye. Just
above her right breast, I think I saw (obviously I didn't want to stare at it
for too long a period) a tattoo of – honest – a tractor. But what really put
me in a good mood for weeks afterwards was my glimpse of the cake. It
was pink and, if I may quote the immortal Kenny Everett, all done in the
worst possible taste. And there you have it: a summary of what I saw as I
opened my eyes. Pink, and in the worst possible taste. The Headquarters
building had been completed only a year or so ago, at a cost of approximately sixty-three million US dollars. It was right on the ocean, with its
own lake and sprawling out over several acres; it was no more than three
stories high, but it was pink and in the worst possible taste.

The next bit is a blur, to be honest. I was shown to my office, where I
met the previous CEO's personal assistant – a slim, rather sophisticated-
looking lady of senior years, who had obviously not slept the previous
night at the thought of what lay ahead of her. I looked into my office, and
was greeted by a huge orange leather sofa. Then I was ushered into the
Big Room where one hundred assorted VPs, SVPs and EVPs[10] looked at
me in silence. They had only known about me for a few days, and the
press had been able to dig up little more than my name and the fact that
I was only forty-two and *managed English pubs*. It was no wonder they
looked at me as though I was ET, and it was no wonder I walked into
the room feeling like Neil Armstrong with his famous 'small steps for
mankind' quip. Time for the speech.

I'm sorry about this, but I have no recollection of what I said at this
seminal event – and I doubt that anybody else present has. I'm half Irish,
so standing up in front of an audience and spouting bullshit comes half
naturally to me – and I filled the room with verbal wallpaper while one
hundred non-listening people eyed me up, and while I tried to return
the compliment. All I can remember is that I have never seen so many
eyes so far out on stalks.

10 Vice Presidents, Senior Vice Presidents, Executive Vice Presidents.

When the speech finished, my boss was out of there at a rather un-dignified speed. The audience dispersed to their assorted offices to wait for what was to come next, and I headed back to my own office. Other than to meet a handful of the most senior people and listen to what they had to say, my plan for the first day was to have no plan. I thought a good place to start would be my office and to have a look at what papers had been left – and to see if there were any day-to-day issues that had been smouldering during the elongated inter-regnum and which needed a fire blanket thrown on them. What I found was that my drawers and cupboards were bare. It had been a fiercely contested acquisition, with Pillsbury shareholders eventually over-ruling the in-place management's beleaguered defence, so my predecessor had just pissed off and cleared his desk. The room was empty apart from a display of ludicrously expensive furniture[11] and, on the wall, a framed copy of the Pillsbury 'Mission and Values' Statement.

Now then. I'm going off on a rant now – and the more sensitive readers may want to skip the next paragraph or so. I hate these pretentious, patronising things. I don't mean 'dislike' or 'have an aversion to', I mean what I say: 'hate'. I have seen and read hundreds. I have even – in my early years – been a party to shaping a few. They usually involve employing some retired English professor, armed with a thesaurus, and asking him/her to come up with some fortune-cookie shorthand which makes the company sound as though it knows where it's going and that the people in it give a shit. Neither is usually true, and I can't remember reading one which wasn't a load of dysfunctional, infinitive-splitting, cosmic wank. If it contained the word 'customercentric' I often had to throw up. What you do as an organisation, and your values (what you stand for), are self-evident in your day to day approach and behaviour – particularly when you think nobody is looking. Neither are what you write down. End of.

OK, rant over. You can pick up again now. The Pillsbury one was a beauty. If they had done a tenth of what they said they would do, and/or stood for a fiftieth of what they said they stood for, I wouldn't have been there. I smiled as I held the frame in my hand. I heard a noise and looked up – and the lady-who-had-been-the-previous-CEO's Personal Assistant was at the door looking at me nervously. I decided to avoid

---

11 The orange sofa had been imported from Italy at a 1987 cost of $25,000. It had been sent back twice for being the wrong orange.

an audible version of my rant, and made a decision. Something told me that this lady would be an ideal aide-de-camp for me and what I was facing, so I gave her my best at-ease-putting Lancashire smile and asked her if she would like to work not for me, but with me. There was a pause while this unexpected approach was digested. The pause was followed by a smile. She certainly would. Sheilia (with an extra 'i') was on board. We were now a team of two, and the show was on the road.

18

A seismic clash

From the day I knew I was heading to Burger King, I had started to find out stuff about the brand. I was given – in secret of course – a cubic ton of paper by our consultants, but I paid scant attention to this as a source. It involved a lot of figures, gleaned from annual reports and a recent history of analyst's published commentaries. For sure, at some stage, I would have to get my head around all this – but there was no point in picking a particular figure out with tweezers and shaping a major policy initiative around its inadequacy until I had actually got my feet under the table, got a team around me and had a acquired a much better idea about the science and the art of the possible. In those early pre-arrival days I was after finding out something much more fundamental. From my very earliest findings it was clear to me that I was to be heading for a seismic culture clash – indeed I knew that, in the eyes of many interested commentators, I would be a manifestation of such a culture clash.

The culture of an organisation – whether business or otherwise – is an odd phenomenon. A while back, in Book One, I noted that for most of my teenage years that I had lived in a place called Ashton-under-Lyne, and that nobody I knew (then or now) knew what a Lyne was or what we were doing under it. The word 'culture', when applied to an organisation, and not something growing in a laboratory, is similarly difficult to pin down. I often heard the Shell-Mex and BP I worked for in the 1960s described as a 'paternalistic' organisation – presumably implying that it was run by kindly, fatherly figures who may, on rare occasions, have to apply tough love, but who generally behaved in a benign fashion while they pottered along addressing the daily tasks at hand. That is so much bollocks. Like every other organisation of any material size I have come across, Shell-Mex and BP had its fair share of shits running their own little empires by fear and generally getting away with it. By contrast, the GrandMet in which I found myself employed when I stood on the threshold of Burger King, was often referred to (in culture shorthand) as a 'hire and fire' organisation. For sure, there was a fairly high managerial churn rate – but that was partly because the company took its time to pick and develop good people and then frequently lost them to other companies who would just lie in wait to headhunt the finished articles. There were, indeed, some ruthless managers in the organisation, but for every one of those I saw, there was a matching executive who gave a damn about his or her people, was fiercely loyal and worked hard at helping subordinates reach their potential.

I was, therefore, confused and suspicious about this whole concept of organisational culture, but I knew I was heading into the mother and father of clashes of something to do with it. Whatever it was, however it manifested itself, my intuition told me that it was going to be a big barrier, and an early barrier, to getting to grips with the task at hand. Instead of just wafting my cap at it, I needed to try and analyse it and figure out a game plan or some game plans.

So – was it going to be about me? Or the two companies? Or the two nations involved? The answer, of course, is that it would be about all three.

It was Mr Spock, in an inspired episode of *Star Trek*, who brought the concept of three-dimensional chess to the attention of the TV-watching world. If you remember, he had three chess boards stacked on top of each other, and would cheerfully move a bishop along its diagonal – *but from one board to another*. If I remember correctly, he didn't lose many games – but the three-dimensional chess board is the best analogy I can come up with to describe the culture clash I faced …

Dimension One

On a personal level, I was everything that everybody looking on didn't expect, particularly those on the other side of the Atlantic. In the UK, particularly in the rapidly changing food and drink industry, it was (just) about becoming accepted that you could employ what many old-stagers saw as a punk rocker to get the job done. I was only forty-two, my hair was too long, I had two university degrees, I did not like status for its own sake and I did not like ostentation. I wore suits, but they were off the peg, from Marks and Spencer. The W Gene lurked inside me, and my humour often just pissed off at angles that nobody – even me – could forecast. I worked hard and long, and played the same, and didn't pay enough attention to my family. It was a long, long way from my first post-university job (back) in Shell as an area representative – where we were the first generation in such positions not to have to carry a hat and gloves.

There were a few (thankfully declining in numbers) in the UK who thought people like me – people who, in their eyes, were barely shaving and who, if not being totally uncouth were a long way from being couth – brought more problems to UK business than we solved. But their time was coming to an end. Thatcher was in power, the Big Bang had hit the city, the long lunch was dead, nationalised industries and state-owned houses were being privatised, and revolution was in the air. The climate for investment was healthy, we could get information quickly and change was wanted fast. I ticked a lot of boxes.

Apart from California's Silicon Valley, where if you were eighteen you were deemed past it, the role model for the CEO of a national or international company in the USA was much more conservative. It was highly likely to be male, mid to late fifties, silver-haired, with a trophy wife and a shed-load of share options. He would be about as restless as a sloth after a heavy petting session which had had ended successfully. He would fly everywhere in the corporate jet, and if he could get a stretch limousine in his office corridor he would use it to go to the bathroom. The wiser and more successful businesses kept his influence to the invitation list for the company's annual sponsorship of a PGA golf event.

That's what the Burger King employees, franchisees, suppliers, investors and most onlookers were expecting. It's not what they needed, but it's what they were expecting – and it was the first dimension of the culture clash I would have to address.

Dimension Two

At a corporate level, GrandMet was about as far away from Pillsbury on a culture spectrum as it was possible to be. Many years later, when my beloved Manchester City finally wrestled the championship away from Manchester United (who seemed to have owned it for about fifty years),

Sir Alex Ferguson, United's manager, described us as 'noisy neighbours' – and there is something in that picture, that idea, that could have applied to GrandMet in the late 1980s. It was noisy, spirited and ambitious. With some justification, the company believed it understood modern brands and branding. It understood that you had to invest in them carefully and professionally – but beyond that you tortured every penny you spent. GrandMet's adolescent growth had been on the back of property. It saw its future growth on the back of brands. It delivered its profit forecast every year without fail – and, if the numbers didn't quite add up to that commitment, it found imaginative (but always legal) ways to make them do so. In short, it was a bit of an upstart company, not showing too much respect for venerable old branded companies (such as Pillsbury) or the views of the more conservative City financial analysts.

Five thousand miles away, Pillsbury was asleep at the wheel. Its main brands – Pillsbury dough products, Burger King Restaurants, Häagen Dazs ice cream and Green Giant vegetables – were undoubtedly powerful brand names but were lying in some sort of hammock idly tossing cash flow at a bunch of uninspired but high maintenance silver-hairs at the assorted palatial corporate centres. Pillsbury had acquired Burger King in the 1970s, and when I arrived the brand had not had a new product launch or a refreshed marketing campaign for a decade. It had of, course, spent that sixty-three million dollars on a new corporate HQ by the sea, possibly so they could all watch it sink into the brand sunset.

It was unthinkable, of course, that a noisy upstart neighbour like GrandMet could unhinge its jaw like a reticulated python and attempt to swallow this established pillar of the world's branded establishment. But it did, and it swallowed it whole – and all those onlookers noted in Dimension One (above) also wondered whether you would be able to see the upcoming clash of corporate cultures in space.

Dimension Three

This shotgun marriage didn't just cause ripples in my personal hinterland and on the pages of business magazines. It hit – and was played up by – the national media on both sides of the Atlantic. At the same time that GrandMet completed the acquisition of the Pillsbury Group, USA's Ford completed the acquisition of Britain's Jaguar motor company. Now *that's* what was supposed to happen – the USA was the all-conquering global business Goliath. In a way, Burger King was a more iconic American brand than Jaguar was in Britain – after all it was about hamburgers, with all that barbeque and western imagery hovering in the middle distance. The fact that a British pub company had triumphed in the multi-billion-dollar arm-wrestle, and were sending an English pub manager over to run it, seemed not only to be inappropriate but incomprehensible to the point of taking the piss. Although Pillsbury was the parent company, it was the takeover of Burger King rather than any of the other brands that got the column inches and TV and radio shrieks.

Now that's culture clash, one that plays out on three dimensions. No pressure there then.

Once I'd analysed it and given it some sort of shape, however, I parked it, took out the keys and left it by the side of the road. I knew where it was, I knew it was a big issue to a lot of people – but I also knew that, with so many people watching, I'd have the chance to make a couple of signals early on which would address some of the clashing issues. Maybe, even, we could see if we could ditch the two-culture potential pissing contest and create a hybrid third-way culture that would help us all get the job done.

I got such a chance early on, within a couple of weeks of starting. We needed a high-impetus US marketing campaign for the brand, and I didn't think we had the guy or gal either in the inherited Burger King team, or available in GrandMet, to deliver. If we could get this right – and we could make a start by getting the right person to do the job – it would go a long way to bridging gaps on all three dimensions. We had a sniff of a top guy, working in the industry for a competitor, who had responded to an initial approach with a guarded agreement to meet and talk. He (understandably) would not/could not come down to our headquarters, so we agreed to meet in a hotel in Orlando, which was on his week's itinerary.

Here's a first glance at what I inherited. I drove to Miami airport and caught the plane to Orlando. When I arrived, I was met by a guy holding a sign up with my name on it. He led me to a stretch limousine. I got in. The car started, and I settled down to do some background reading on the guy we were meeting. I hadn't even found my papers when the car stopped. We were at the *Airport Marriott*. I could almost have got in the back of the limo, crawled to the front and got out and been at my destination. We had hired a limo and a driver for about three hundred metres. You couldn't make it up.

We got our man, and I had a chance to give off two of the culture-changing signals I mentioned above:

1. We were able to announce that we had put in place one of the USA's best and respected food service brand marketing guys. At stroke we signalled that we were not here to drain cash, but to invest in and get behind the brand. We would be anything but asleep at the wheel. At a personal, corporate and national level, a lot of folk started looking through different lenses.

2. Second signal? At my weekly 'Town Hall' meeting with my head-quarter staff, I told them, smiling, of my Orlando limousine comedy. Cue lots of laughter. Still smiling, I banned all limos. We needed to cut costs, but at the same time we needed to invest in the brand. We would, therefore, spend our money where it would benefit the brand most, which would not be on limousines to and from airports. In future? Jump in a cab. Cue for laughter dying off a bit, but a lot of thoughtful faces.

I got another chance for another signal at about the same time – and I'll use it to illustrate some of the dafter practices going on before we arrived. The Burger King top management structure was that about ten people reported to the CEO directly, some on the Board of Directors, some co-opted to the Executive Committee. If you were in this gold-plated group and you moved office (either on appointment or through a job change) you were given a budget to decorate and furnish your office. Now, remember this was in 1989. That budget was *fifty thousand* US dollars.

The guy (poor guy!) who was running US operations and who I in-herited was just setting of on one of these projects for his office when I arrived, so I let it run. I watched and listened (he was next door) as this hard-bodied, big-haired, super-model female interior designer arrived one day and 'worked with him' to come up with a design and furnishing plan. I bit my tongue. Over the next couple of weeks, it happened. Ar-mies of painters and carpet layers and then furniture providers trooped in and then – dah dah – it was ready. I had a look. *Everything* was white. Walls, flooring, desk, chairs, sofa, occasional table, blinds, pens, pen-cils.[12] Everything. White.

12 Sorry, I got carried away. Not pencils. I made that up.

Now, guess who (or what) makes an appearance? It's the W Gene!! Things had gone fairly well for me in the first couple of weeks, but the W Gene couldn't resist risking sliding the whole thing down a snake. When my man was out of the office one afternoon, I got a NoBo chart pad sheet, and with a large red felt-tip pen I wrote the following on it:

DADE COUNTY
EMBALMING CLINIC

I then pinned it on his door and waited. I never actually heard anything in terms of formal feedback from him or anybody, but the $50,000 per office decorating and furnishing policy self-destructed right there and right then. And there was a second learning experience for all sides: whatever the dimensions of your culture clash, if you play it sparingly, and you have the W Gene popping its head over the parapet from time to time, an occasional laugh can help you bridge it.

Bit by bit, the issues became less on each chessboard, but they never disappeared completely. As the time passed and the company's results improved, many of the daft prejudices – on both sides – dissolved, but you cannot completely turn water into wine. All parties retained an innate ability to piss the others off when things seemed to be going smoothly.

Here's one example – and it's a gem. There is a sensitivity to race and gender issues in the USA that will never be *completely* understood – and, indeed, accepted – in the UK. The gap and clash is way, way smaller now than it was in the late 1980s, and in some ways we did our best to keep it alive and kicking for a while longer than it would and should have done. About a year or so into this shotgun marriage, the London-based GrandMet warlords decided to have a group-wide senior management conference. The second decision was that it would be in London, so well over fifty US-based senior managers, of mixed race and gender, flew into London for a couple of days of bonding.

Strike One: at the Gala Dinner, Allen Sheppard was a bit tardy in arriving for his speech, and cheerfully explained the delay as being because 'there was a hot and cold running maid in my room'. It's not actually very funny, but it was the sort of boys'-school humour that went down well on these sorts of black-tie occasions in the City at the time. The effect it had on the American female senior managers present was instant and impressive: they froze. And they froze in coiled positions, ready to bite.

Strike Two: you'd have difficulty making this one up. In the next day's presentation by the head of GrandMet's drinks business,[13] he illustrated a point he was making about the need to be local in your marketing by screening a slide consisting of a photograph of a very black Zulu-type warrior. He was in full headdress and loincloth, *and was waving a spear.* The African-American USA senior management contingent, understandably, staged their own Boston Tea party.

The Third Strike? Back to yours truly.

Humour, and its ability to bring people together, is a massive potential tool in dealing with culture clashes – but it can go very wrong. Americans have a very different sense of humour to Brits (they hated Monty Python but loved Benny Hill) and they don't really appreciate surreal stuff coming at them from unlikely angles. I won more than I lost, but occasionally got it wrong. At my first gala dinner with Burger King's senior management, I was to give the after-dinner speech. Now, I have always been a fan of *Private Eye*[14], and in particular Peter Cook's early contributions. He used to write in to the letters column as Sir Hubert Gussett (ret'd), railing at anything modern. In one letter he came out with the immortal phrase 'My dear lady wife, whose name temporarily escapes me…'. I loved it so much that, like all good plagiarists, I stole it, and used it to lighten up the introduction to my after-dinner speech. Judy, who was sitting next to me on the top table, gave one of her corporate smiles[15] and the evening rolled on. It was only the next day I found out that I had been reported to my own Human Resource Director by one of my own management – for anti-feminism.

This caused a bit of a procedural problem as I was Chairman and CEO of the Company, and therefore the end of the line in the disciplinary process. So I had to take myself aside and give myself a formal oral warning. I can't say it was better than a Doncaster Left-Hander, but in its own way it was quite fulfilling.

Did all parties ever completely blend? No, we didn't. There was never a complete acceptance on the USA side of the Atlantic that this latest

13 This was IDV. After the merger with Guinness (with their Distillers drinks business) it became Diageo, the global drinks giant that is the modern day iteration of GrandMet.
14 The UK satirical magazine.
15 Which is the equivalent of a Tiger Woods 1000-yard stare.

manifestation of the Mayflower and its Pilgrims (and notably its head Pilgrim – me) was wanted or needed. But in our first full year of trading, as a three-dimensional forced-marriage of cultures, our same-store sales rose by five per cent. It's amazing how success shuts some people up.

19

Leader of the pack

There are two things I didn't want this book to be.

First – a 'womb to tomb' autobiography, covering what Holden Caulfield[16] noted as 'All that David Copperfield kind of crap'. They are only for people of enormous public or self interest, and I am neither. I actually bore myself, so some Lord only knows what I do to others. My point in doing this is to capture (three times) a time, place, a cast of characters and set of circumstances which *are* of interest – and to be the narrator. A bit like that guy who wanders across the stage in *Blood Brothers*.

The second thing I didn't want this to be is a business book. The last time I was in Waterstones there were about three acres devoted to all things business, and the arrival of yet another Tom Peters-Lite is not high on the planet's desperate needs at the moment.

If I'm going to do the qualified job I set out to do, however, I need to drift dangerously close to the second of these. To tell the story of those few years in Burger King you need to know something about the business we were in, and something about what I stand for and what I do when somebody pins a leadership badge on me.

Let's do the easy one first – the business. If you ask a hundred people what they think Burger King Corporation does, ninety nine of them

---

16 J. D. Salinger – *Catcher in the Rye*. If you've not read it, go to your nearest good bookshop, pick it up and buy a coffee. This bit's on the first page – one of the great first pages in literature.

would assume that the clue is in the name – and reply that they sell burgers. And they would be so wrong.

The business of Burger King Corporation is to sell *franchises*, and there is a world of difference. If you sell a burger, like any other physical product, that represents a finished deal. If you sell two of them next year, you are showing growth and so on and so on. If you sell a franchise, it is not a finished deal on the day of the transaction – you then receive *twenty years* of income during the life of the franchise agreement. It is a partnership: the franchisor invests in developing and controlling the brand, and the franchisee invests in the retail outlet, the products, the staff and all the other stuff needed to ensure the branded product reaches the end user.

What could possibly go wrong? Well, in Burger King's case, in the 1980s, pretty much everything – all of which was manifested in that awful Burger King I went into on US1 in Miami before my first day on the job. The temptation for the franchisor, once you have a critical mass of franchised outlets (each providing twenty years of cash flow) is to carefully insert your thumb up your backside and do as little as possible on the 'development and control' of the brand while at the same time building pink palaces for the headquarters staff. In the meantime, the franchisees – taking careful note that the brand is not being developed and/or controlled – develop an attitude that results in them turning their attentions away from competing on their local streets and aiming huge arcs of urine at the pink palaces in question.

Now, I know that was a bit technical – with thumbs up backsides and arcs of urine lighting up the night sky – but that's all you need to know for the purpose of this book. The alternative would be to provide an appendix with endless, *endless* analyses, figures and graphs – which is what I had to plough through before I reached the above conclusions. I was being handed a tired brand, one which was being milked, and wich had pissed-off franchisees.

OK, now onto the difficult bit: me. It was clear to everybody that change was needed, that change was imminent, and that I would be the leader of that change. In a perfect world, as I entered onto this cluttered stage, I would have made it crystal clear what I *stood for,* and then what I was going to *do.* I found the second much easier than the first.

I have the same problems with personal value statements that I do with corporate ones. To write them down, or trumpet them in any way, strikes me as self-serving and a bit like a sophisticated Business Plan. I've seen thousands of man-hours spent on Business Plans, and you know that, when you present it, it represents the one scenario than you can *guarantee* will not occur. At the time of writing I'm watching the new head of Barclays in the UK spouting to anybody that will listen about the new values that both he and the company will stand for – but, to me, it's only after the event that you can cast an eye on somebody's attitude, behaviour and achievements and say that that is what he/she stood for.

So, I couldn't, and didn't, do it then. I can look back, and have a go now and – for starters – I can tell you what I didn't stand for.

I have never been comfortable with totally laissez-faire capitalism. Somehow, Adam Smith arrived at Gordon Gecko, and I simply do not buy that earnings per share driven by the winds of greed can be the only success criteria for commerce. But, then again, I find it difficult to hang my hat on any simplistic hook designed to explain why we do what we do. In the 1960s, Theodore ('Ted') Levitt wrote that the only purpose for being in business was to 'secure and retain a customer' – and you would not believe how many CEOs I have heard pay lip service to this maxim in my years in business. And not one of them believed it. To the vast majority of CEOs a 'customer' is a monetary unit that represents the difference between an incremental unit of revenue and an incremental unit of costs. Of course they don't believe Levitt's fortune-cookie commandment, and they are right not to do so, because it's bollocks.

Looking back over my own approach, after the event, I got my first clue from the world of golf. It was Phil Mickleson who sowed the seeds of an idea when he said 'The object of golf is not to win. It is to play like a gentleman *and win*'.

Now, forget the 'gentleman' bit – if you have ploughed through this book so far you will know by now that that's a coat that will not fit me – but let's play with the idea. I like winning, and I have won (in business) more than I have lost. But the idea of winning *with qualifications* intrigues me. How about this?

The object of business is not to win but to care about those whose lives are affected by your business –
AND WIN.

It probably gets as close as I can to reflecting my own approach to business, a picture painted with the benefit of hindsight. But it's still not quite enough. Who are 'those affected'? To throw (my version of) light on this, I need Margaret Thatcher. No, I am not an unqualified fan of her memory as I don't do binary, doctrinal politics – but there is a quote that rings true in many areas of life. It is one that got her into hot water, although I suspect she wouldn't have lost a lot of sleep over that. She said 'There's no such thing as Society' and anyone vaguely to the left of Tamerlane started frothing and shrieking. Where they got it wrong was that the quote was taken out of context – what she went on to say was that this 'Society' thing was actually made up of *people*. People with names and families and jobs and tensions and successes and… well, you get the picture. And it helped me finish my look back.

So, who are those whose lives are affected by your business? I don't depersonalise it:

- I don't believe in a market. I believe in people who buy your stuff for a wide range of personal reasons.

- I don't believe in a workforce. I believe in people who allocate (maybe) a third of their lives to your cause, and whose rewards for so doing govern their quality of life and security.

- I don't believe in a supply chain. I believe in people whose skills, resources and time make sure you get what you need.

- I don't believe in distributors (agents, franchisees). I believe in people without whose efforts and involvement your stuff wouldn't reach those in Category One above.

- I don't believe in a stock market. I believe in people who have had enough faith in what you do to have put their money where their mouths are.

- I don't believe in communities. I believe in people whose lives can be collaterally damaged (or enhanced) by the side effects of you doing what you do.

So that's who they pinned the troop leader's badge on – a guy who was driven to win, but not at any cost. A guy who, unashamedly, liked to reap the rewards of victory, but did not define the latter in one-dimensional terms.

Did I get the Win? If you look at the first part of the categories (above) – the de-personalised collective descriptors I don't believe in

– then the answer is probably 'yes'. Not one of those was worse off after my time on the bridge. Using the obvious criteria – the revenues and the state of the brand – then it was a successful turnaround. But if you look at the second part – where we home in on the individuals in the crowd – the answer is much muddier. There are individuals in each category, some of whom I can see clearly if I close my eyes, who were collateral damage en route to the trophy ceremony.

Did I *win*, dammit? Answer the bloody question and stop wafting your cap at it. On my terms and looking my shaving mirror, the answer is 'no'. If I was daft enough to attempt a lap of honour, it is the faces of those people I hurt that I would see in the crowd.

With hindsight, therefore, it seems that they appointed a cross between Hamlet and Lou Reed as leader, but appoint me they did. Now we need to sort out what a leader does.

There was a time when the leaders of big businesses started in the ranks and progressed by retaining their front-line skills and adding the new necessary ones as the personal and business growth challenges evolved. Terry Leahy joined Tesco in the junior ranks and grew with it, and then it grew with him. Many reckon that Bill Gates, who founded Microsoft, was still the best code-writer on the company's books when it had become (effectively) the world's operating system. I think they may be the last of a kind.

The required leadership skills in big business today, particularly if it crosses national boundaries, are so wide-ranging, *but with each one so specialist*, that the all-rounder can't hack it anymore. Effective global leaders limit themselves to doing three things brilliantly:

1. Being the masthead nailed to the front of the ship. He or she is who everybody sees – and makes a judgement about the company by interpreting their attitude and behaviour.

2. Tom Peters once said that 'If you got more than one priority, you got none'. I love his work, but that is bollocks – but only in the number quoted. If he had said between three and five, I would have forgiven the grammatical nightmare. In my view, it is the leader's job to listen and be advised – and then take the decisions about *what* the company actually does. Simple.

3. Once the 'what' has been decided, it is the leader's job to decide 'who' does the 'what'. You need the best in the specialist fields needed. And

then, guess what? Once these people are in place, and clear about the 'what' – *get out of the fucking way*. This only works if you genuinely have the balls to delegate the ability to fail.

So, that's who I was at the time, and that's all I had to do. No pressure there then.

20

Who's who?

First, the good news. I inherited *one* person from the in-place Burger King team who was a perfect fit for the job we saw ahead. He was the Chief Counsel, Roger Thompson, and his attitude and capability was crucial in helping me assimilate the differences in the legal environment I was now operating in. In the UK, I was CEO of a retail business with thirty thousand direct employees – and we had one part-time lawyer on the books who doubled as Company Secretary. In Burger King, we had *twenty-five* in-house lawyers – and, about six weeks into the journey, I was thinking it wasn't enough. Of course, franchising is more complex than direct retailing, as is trading in nearly fifty countries – but nothing prepared me for the stultifying, onerous and at times puerile legal hoops you had to go through to do or react to anything. As I got to understand business in the USA, I found that the ongoing position of almost every corporate attorney I met was to put forward six reasons why whatever it was you were thinking of doing wouldn't work – and the good news was that I inherited the one in a thousand that was much more positive.

He was also the guy who, more than once, stopped my W Gene from landing us with a class action lawsuit against us. I think this role ended up taking a fair chunk of his time. On my first day in the office, sometime about mid-afternoon, a smart young man appeared in my doorway – an event which surprised me in itself, as Sheilia had already made it clear that it was in her self-defined job description that she would lay down her life rather than let any unauthorised person into my inner sanctum. It was, apparently, a routine event – at this time each day a paralegal would call in and collect my out-tray to give it to my Chief Counsel for legal vetting. I gave off another signal for everybody to digest, and told him (politely; it was not his fault) to return to wherever he came from. If I was capable of being CEO, I was capable of writing my own letters. This did not deter my Chief Counsel in the slightest. He just found other ways – quite happily and with a smile on his face – to keep me in check, and probably saved us a billion dollars in so doing. On occasions, however, my W Gene caught him in that dreaded position for a lawyer – in the seat of indecision.

As you would imagine, the Pink Palace had a boardroom big enough to have staged a Beatles concert in 1964. It had a chandelier that could be seen from space, and it had a boardroom table that simply defied belief. It was huge and had an exquisite marble top – and I never gathered up the courage to ask where it came from and what it cost. It was so big that you could not reach across it to shake hands (which may have been part of the design brief), and as there were usually only eight or ten of us, we sort-of huddled up one end.

Most of our agendas were filled with mind-numbing procedural and legal stuff, and I would sit staring gloomily down the runway that doubled as a table. I would try everything to keep myself interested – or, at least, looking interested. Often I would stare at an agenda item and ponder 'what would the Lone Ranger do?' but sometimes even that wouldn't work. One day we were reviewing the nightmare legal award against McDonalds – a woman had been awarded a multi-million-dollar ruling because she had spilt her drive-thru coffee on her lap as she drove away from the restaurant and scalded herself. As if we had nothing better to do, we fannied about for about forty minutes on 'should we or shouldn't we do something' – and then the Lone Ranger (or the W Gene, take your pick) came to the rescue: my decision was that we would get our (coffee) cup manufacturers to write the following on the bottom of all our cups:

THIS COFFEE IS HOT, AS YOU INTENDED IT TO BE.
IF YOU SPILL IT ON YOUR GENITALS
YOU DO SO AT YOUR OWN RISK

We didn't. My 'decision' got cut off at the pass by my Chief Counsel, but to this day I am sure he didn't know whether I meant it or not. The reason I am sure is that I don't know either.

So, I had another guy in place – on top of the Financial Controller and Head of Human Resources, GrandMet guys who came in with me. The rest of the inherited senior management had, thoughtfully, as part of the 'defence' against the contested acquisition bid by GrandMet, awarded themselves a generous self-triggering pay-off which would last a year after any acquisition completion. I got most of them to trigger it sooner rather than later – in most cases by adding a few more zeroes on the cheque. If they were to hang about, they would have been part of the problem, not the solution.

If you remember from a previous chapter, and the episode of the 300-metre limousine rent, we had gone for a top marketing guy – and it turns out we landed him. Gary Langstaff was (still is!) his name, but he answered to the nickname 'Ratso'[17] to all who knew him. He was about 5' 5" wherever you measured him, and I remember looking at him during the interview – in the Marriott Hotel at Orlando Airport – and becoming fixated on the fact that, when he sat on the bed, his feet didn't reach the ground. But what he lacked in physical stature he more than made up for in everything else, and he was to play a huge part in the brand's renaissance.

Gary was also the most politically incorrect guy I have ever met, and I've visited all five continents. Sometimes, our exchanges in the privacy of our offices would have made a Regimental Sergeant Major blush – a kind of standard greeting from me to him would be 'Hey, Ratso, how are Snow White and the other six?' He would barely pause before launching a verbal surface-to-groin missile my way that would be unpublishable, even here. He swore more than I did, sometimes whacking a swear word in the middle of words he deemed too long to be without one.[18] He wore his heart on his sleeve, was immensely skilled at – and loved – what he did and had no time for what he saw as false protocols. The Garys of this world are an endangered species, and business is all the worse for it.

At the outcome, Allen Sheppard had told me that the Burger King challenge was the one that all the commentators would be watching. It wasn't as big as Pillsbury in numbers, but it was bigger in profile and was perceived to be in a worse state. It was the one they thought we couldn't do. Allen told me – a statement reinforced by my US boss – that I could

17 From the role immortalised by Dustin Hoffman in *Midnight Cowboy*.
18 I think 'elecfuckingtricity' was a one of his. If not, apologies – but there were many others.

'take my pick' from available senior GrandMet staff as I put my team together. In fact, once the secret was out (if you remember, a while before
I actually left) I suddenly became immensely popular with a bunch of
guys who fancied coming on the expeditionary force with me. But there
was only one I really wanted.

Christopher Dams was responsible for the supply chain in my UK
Empire. He was a veteran of the UK supply chain business. For sure, the
supply chain companies would have different names and the numbers
would be bigger in the USA, but the principles would be the same and
I saw his skills as eminently transferable. It was not just this I wanted,
however; he brought something else to the party. You don't build an
effective team with lookalikes and thinkalikes, and Christopher was a
great foil for me. His thoughts were linear, whereas mine were angled.
His logic complemented my unpredictability – but most of all his Rightness Gene worked well with my W Gene.

I'm not talking about a moral compass, but many business decisions
fail a basic 'Test of Rightness'. Example? A couple of years later, when
things were going well for us, it became clear that Pillsbury were not
going to make their forecast year-end figures – and would, therefore,
jeopardise the whole of GrandMet's ability to do so. We in Burger King
were on track – but we also had the ability to create a one-off profit by
selling profitable company-run restaurants to franchisees. It was a classic 'selling off the family silver to pay the butler', but we did it. Hey-ho,
GrandMet made its figures and all was 'well'. But it wasn't, because in
the next year we were starting with a smaller base and (therefore) had to
make even more – which probably meant selling off even more profitable assets. If you scrape away the slightest surface of that, it is a dick
decision and that's what I mean by businesses failing the Test of Rightness. And it's the kind of check and balance against that sort of attitude
and behaviour he brought to the party's thinking.

Very early on we faced a supply-chain lawsuit. We had an in-house
distribution business which we ran at arm's length – but which compet-
ed in some markets with distribution businesses owned by franchisees.
It was not an ideal long-term solution, but one which we inherited, and
which we kept going because it enabled us to offer a well run and com-
petent distribution service (ours) in every market. Then one of the franchisee owner-distributors sued us, the basis being that we were unfairly
competitive against his business.

I could see this being very deflective and providing a lot of people with 'I told you so' ammunition if we let it go to court and suffered a high-profile defeat. I can't remember in exact detail the conversation I had with Chris on this, but I think it went something like this:

Me: We are being sued.

Him: Yes.

Me: I don't like it.

Him: Yes.

Me: What do you mean 'yes'?

Him; Yes, you don't like it.

Me: Jesus. You and your 'yesses'...

Him: Yes.

Me: Look we are on a hiding to nothing.

Him: Yes.

Me: We have nothing to gain and a ton to lose.

Him: Yes.

Me: I don't even want to *be* in distribution long term.

Him: Yes.

Me: Plus plus plus – it's an American court, with an American business suing a UK business that nobody likes, and one they all think should be taught a lesson.

Him: Yes.

Me: So, do we go to court?

Him: Yes.

Me: Why? Why on earth would you do that as long as you have a hole in your bottom?

Him: *Because it's the right thing to do.*

We went to court. Both of us. Our (inherited) operation was found technically guilty, but only on a minor technicality, and we paid out nominal damages – and (the big win) we were given the right to carry on offering an in-house distributor service, strangely enough to the happiness and benefit of many other franchisees.

I slept like a baby that night. We had done something right, and won the day. You need all sorts in a team, but if you can land a talent that (apart from any specialist skills) can constantly check and balance you against the Test of Rightness, you are so much stronger. I got that in Chris Dams, and the core of my team was now in place.

21
Just do it

So, we had a leader in place (with attitude) and the core of a team. It was about time we did something about this troubled[19] brand. I've mentioned before that I had pages and pages of analysis and commentary about its problems before I arrived; on the plane coming over from the UK I measured the depth of the papers analysing the 'troubles' and it came to two and a half inches. I seemed that the troubles had more constituent parts than my childhood Airfix Bismarck kit.

That was, of course, before I got there. Once I had my feet under the desk, there was a long and permanent queue outside my door to tell me about more troubles, as though my office was the water at Lourdes.

One of the great sins of modern business – brought on by the ability to create infinite information – is to over-analyse. In fairness I read all this stuff, and listened to all the whingeing, and then I asked my favourite source for a distilled version of the troubles. That source was the IBO,[20] and it came up with the following paragraph:

The brand has a tired image and offering; the franchisees are not making enough returns; the supply chain is amateur night; the international[21] business is a sitcom and the management is top heavy.

---

19 I must have read this adjective a thousand times. *Everybody* called this brand 'troubled'. I began to think the brand was called Troubled Burger King, just as I thought my beloved soccer team were called Manchester City Nil in the 1960s.
20 The Institute of the Bleedin' Obvious.
21 i.e. Non-USA business.

There you go: five points, thirty-three words. In no way does this minimise the size and range of the troubles, it just simplifies what we had to do in a way that was digestible. The business schools would call the five points the Key Leverage Variables – in other words the areas where we would get the most bang for our effort-buck. What they told me was that pretty much everything we did should be about improving the start position in one or more of them.

You will notice that I have not included 'low profits' as one of the troubles. They were indeed low – in fact they were non-existent – but they were not one of the troubles. They were the *result* of all of the troubles. Four days into the job I got my first forecast of the current year's 'profits': we were already in January and the year would finish in September – and we were on track to lose $90 million for the full year. The day after that, my boss arrived for a follow-up meeting, and I asked him what the GrandMet warlords were expecting. He didn't say anything, but scribbled something down on a bit of paper and passed it over the table: a (pre-tax) *profit* of $110 million. That was just a swing of $200 million in about nine months. Many thought we should get some consultants in urgently, and spend half a million dollars on a really detailed plan to deliver that goal. I didn't.

In this whole area of planning I am a big fan of Carl von Clausewitz, who laid down his pearls of wisdom on the subject nearly two hundred years ago.[22] His premise was that detailed planning always failed due to the inevitable frictions encountered, chance events, imperfections in execution and the independent will of the opposition. Instead, you should rely on 'human elements': leadership, morale and the almost instinctive savvy of the best generals. None of the Prussian leaders expected a plan of operations to survive beyond the first contact with the enemy. They set only the broadest of objectives and emphasised seeing unforeseen opportunities as they arose. Strategy was not a lengthy action plan; it was the evolution of a few central ideas through continually changing circumstances.

That was the approach I wanted – almost applying the W Gene to business planning. I was sure we could do it, but we probably wouldn't know all the details on 'how' it was to be achieved until we looked back after the event.

I'm nearly at the end of the Tom Peters-Lite bit, and I'll finish it with a few bullet points summarising what we did to improve our base position in each of the five target areas:

22 *On War*, Carl von Clausewitz, first published 1832

The brand had a tired image and offering

- Within a year, Ratso hit the market with Burger King's first new advertising campaign for a decade.

- New products were introduced (also the first for a decade) to attract women and kids. Previously, the brand had figured its targeted audience to be 'Bubba' – a blue-collar American male aged between sixteen and twenty-five. We needed to get the women and kids back from McDonalds.

- The existing field management resources were split – half to be 'business consultants' to the franchisees, and half to focus on the correct day to day delivery of the brand.

- Some high-profile but poorly performing franchisees were bought out.

The franchisees were not making enough returns

- Another Brit followed me from GrandMet UK – David Fitzjohn. He 'value-engineered' the set-up cost of a new Burger King unit (land and buildings) down from (about) $1 million to $600,000.

- The advertising and new products grew store revenues.
- Without reducing quality, we reduced products' cost (see supply chain, below)

- These three improvements made a hell of a difference to franchisee economics – and all of a sudden franchises started to sell themselves. New franchisees could see that you could make money again, and existing franchisees wanted more of the same. In August 1991, the *Miami Herald* was able to report 'Franchisees applaud company's new efforts'. In November 1991, *Adweek* wrote that 'Burger King does it the franchisees' way'. Neither had written sentences like that for a long time.

The supply chain was amateur night

- Chris Dams revolutionised the supply chain. Instead of an eternal pissing contest between franchisees and the company as to who should buy and distribute product, we set up an independent and professional supply-chain company to do both. The whole thing was invented one night in my home kitchen and was an alchemic blend of his Test of Rightness and my W Gene. Within two years this had taken about two to three per cent off front-line product costs. And all the bickering stopped.

The international business was a sitcom

- We faced problems on two fronts here. First, The US franchisees my-opically felt any non-USA development of the brand was a waste of time, effort and resources that could (and should) have been invested in them. Paradoxically, we felt that the real growth potential of the brand was outside the USA. We needed to give a signal, both to the USA and to potential international franchisees, that this is where the future lay – and we spent multi-millions of dollars in acquiring the Wimpy brand in the UK and converting their prime sites to Burger King. That woke a lot of people up to what was happening and what was going to happen.

- The second problem was that every existing international franchise we had was in some sort of trouble. Some were just the wrong people who had taken on the brand for the wrong reasons; others were at sea with poor support, inadequate supply chains and non-existent mar-keting. Again, a signal was needed, and we recruited a heavyweight – Freddy Dellis, another European – to focus entirely on our inter-national business to right the existing wrongs and start the journey (which is still going on today) to develop the brand's international potential.

The management was top heavy

- I sat down with the personnel manual one day, at home over a long cold drink, and discovered an outstanding fact: if you followed one line of command, there were *thirteen* layers of management between me and somebody who bought a Whopper sandwich. These guys had job descriptions supposedly matching accountability and responsibility, and giving them decision-taking powers. What a crock. The W Gene kicked in and a papal edict went out that we needed to get to a position FAST where the layers of management between me and a customer could fit comfortably in a mid-sized family car. It was seen by the deliberately blind just as a cost-cutting exercise, and I will not pretend for a minute that there was no collateral damage in the form of hurt families and damaged careers on the way, but it was primarily about giving us an organisational structure that was both effective and efficient. It was designed to help us improve the start position in all five target areas – nothing more, nothing less. For those who keep a note of these things, the ancient Chinese Army – where hierarchical command was effectively invented – never had more than ten layers.

So, there you have it. This chapter runs to only about 1600 words, and a chunk of them are down to Clausewitz. It sounds simple, and it was – although that belies the massive efforts that so many people put in. In my fourth year at the helm I had a letter from American Airlines advising me that I had accumulated three million frequent flyer miles, enough to get me an upgrade to fly business class to Mars (if they ever free it up at a time when I want to go). Simple is not the same as easy.

We made our $110 million scribbled on that little bit of paper. By June 1991, the *Miami Herald* noted we had increased *again* by sixteen per cent, and the *Wall Street Journal* reported that our strong results had helped lift the 'UK Concern's earnings'.

Bingo.

22
King Billy BB

I need to start this part with two qualifications:

- It is about – and aimed at – males. But not completely …
- 'Fame' is not quite the right word, but it will do while I get the boat away from the pier.

It was Kevin Bacon, the actor famously connected to everybody on the planet via six joined dots, who said 'Show me an actor who doesn't want to be famous and I'll show you a liar'. For a period of my life I had a high public profile and came across a lot of folk who also had one, and I would not only endorse that sentiment but also add to it. I would extend it to athletes, entertainers, business warlords and pretty much anyone who sports a penis.

The concept of 'fame' differs amongst those groups, and I need to peel a layer or two off the surface definition before I can make the points I want to. It was Sam Ellis (that's the Sam Ellis of Book One) who clarified it for me. Fifty years after our school days finished he was in his umpteenth football management job after a successful professional playing career that included him playing in a Wembley Cup Final in front of 100,000 people. A northern (English) newspaper had picked up that we were both from the same school and had written a piece on it. Having lived in that strange goldfish bowl for nearly half a century, Sam made the point that our two fields of 'fame' were different in one simple way:

footballers, like all athletes and entertainers *sign autographs*, whereas business warlords rarely do. A case in point is that when Sir Alex Ferguson retired from Manchester United the world's media dedicated about half its content to his passing in the following week. At almost the same time, Paul Walsh, who had taken up the reins at Pillsbury when I went to Burger King and who went on to run Diageo, stepped down to the accolades of the business world but with little media coverage outside the financial pages. Manchester United's market value is just over £1 billion. Paul *added* £13 billion to Diageo's value during his time at the helm. The audiences are different – but beyond that many of the principles (and consequences) are the same.

I have known some people, of both sexes, who are simply comfortable with, and in, fame – but with the majority (and I include myself), something happens to them. For my purposes I needed an adjunct to the simple word 'famous' to get a handle on it.

I am indebted to our youngest son, Ben, for the clinical definition of the state I am looking to describe. It came after one of the players of our beloved Manchester City was reported in the media for some piece of asinine behaviour – not long after a good spell in our team had seen him awarded an international cap. Suddenly he was rarely out of the headlines for some off-piste activity or other. After yet another episode, Ben and I were digesting the paparazzi coverage of our hero, and Ben simply summed him up: 'The problem is he thinks he's Billy Big Bollocks.'

Billy Big Bollocks. BBB for short. A perfect crystallised description of the state of mind just beyond fame – and one I drifted in and out of for a while.

I am not a man of faith or Faith[23] – a fact I regret, as it must sometimes make life's snakes and ladders much easier to handle. However, I do find it hard to believe that everything ends as you draw your life's last breath. I am sure that there must be some kind of exit interview and, if there is, I am also sure there will be a section consisting of two linked questions:

1. Did you, at any time, experience a degree of fame in your life? (If the answer is no, go straight on to the next section – the one that asks if you knew Jimmy Savile.)

---

23 There's a big difference if it starts with a capital F.

2. If your answer is yes, can you pinpoint the exact time when you became Billy Big Bollocks?

I think I can.

It is hard for people outside big business to understand the machinations of corporate PR. It is a complex mixture of science and art, and of pro-action and re-action. If there's bad news about, there's a frantic corporate search for (what we in GrandMet called) 'sparklers' – bits of good news that can be sexed up and then flared into the night sky of the media to distract attention from the doomy and gloomy bit. An unplanned sparkler is a very rare thing.

After a year or so of us at the helm, things were going well for the Burger King brand, and there was a pretty constant call from London for us to come up with another sparkler or two. A lot of it was activity oriented – a new product launch, a new country entry, a new acquisition, a new recruitment – but both our London and in-house Burger King PR teams knew there was a story around me as well. The unconventional Limey pub manager seemed to be overseeing the awakening of a brand that had been sleeping, and sleeping despite the best efforts of a conventional gaggle of Corporate America's finest. As a result, quite a few of our sparklers moved from being activity based and became centred around me.

An effective and efficient PR team is based on its contacts and its networking ability, and to land a Big One takes time and (frequently unrewarding) hard work. My guys had a bee their bonnets about getting the Burger King success story into *Fortune* magazine – and eventually won their equivalent of the lottery. You can see the cover overleaf. This is the date that I will enter into my exit interview form as the day I became BBB. For the outsider, it is quite easy to spot the symptoms – but when you yourself are in a BBB state of mind it is quite hard to identify them until it's too late. If you are in doubt about yourself, or somebody you know, here are three symptoms that almost always signal the disease:

You wink at yourself

This does not necessarily involve the closing and re-opening of an eye – but it does reflect a mindset. The genesis of identifying this as a symptom came to me many years ago, care of a fellow board member of a company I was working for, while we were on a business trip to Hamburg.

Enter stage right: Billy Big Bollocks

With the business of the day completed, we headed off as a group with the aim, in some cases, to paint the town. As we regrouped the following morning, quite a few of the group looked as though they had been hit by a Volvo. One of them, it transpired, had hit the red light district and been with a prostitute.

I have never been with a prostitute, but I am not a prude. Provided (and it is a big proviso) there is no coercion, and that both sides of the supply and demand curve are free to agree on the whys, wherefores and price, the planet's oldest profession is OK by me. What made this one memorable, however, was our guy's post-match interview with the rest of us on the morning after. Apparently, the room where the action took place was heavily appointed with mirrors and, at some juncture, our hero caught sight of his own reflection, and *winked at himself*.[24]

To wink at your own reflection – physically or metaphorically – can only be the result of a BBB state of mind. Did I evidence these symptoms? On reflection, I can think of a hundred examples – but how about this one for a gem? At one time, not long after my dinner 'with' the Queen, I was back in England on a short visit, and I found myself mentally preparing my *Desert Island Discs* list. Just in case.

You acquire for effect

I read somewhere that a minimum of ninety per cent of the acquisitions made by the male of the species are made with a view as to the *effect* they will have on other people. My only thought on that is that it is a bit low – but if and when you reach BBB status there is no longer a doubt. You crash into the hundred per cent barrier.

I don't like ostentation, but this is a different trait. Somewhere around 1990, I acquired a first-generation mobile phone – about the size of the foundation stone for the average Greek temple – the minute it became available. I strode everywhere with it glued to my ear, but with nobody on the other of the line for the simple reason that nobody else had one. The clear effect on everybody was that I was a mover and a shaker, or so I thought. In hindsight, I now know they were thinking: BBB.

The phone was not my best in this category – that was clearly the purchase of a pair of braces.[25] These were not the ones for my teeth, but the ones that go over your shoulders to keep your trousers up. This was the Gordon Gecko era, and the look that went with it was de rigueur for all aspiring BBBs. I had always used a simple belt for the job of trouser suspension, and yet – incredibly – one day I found myself addressing one of my Headquarter 'Mass Meetings' in a blue and white pin-striped shirt and a newly acquired pair of braces. As the text-messagers say: WTF.

You become a parody of yourself

If the first two are a bit flippant, this is serious. The first two are super-

---

24 On reflection, it's one thing doing that and it is another to report back that you did it. That is serious BBB.

25 Suspenders to Americans.

ficial; they come and go, they don't really affect your ability to do your job – but this one does. You begin to parody yourself.

You achieve something on the back of a number of factors: luck, skill, timing, ambition, mentors, greed (etc., etc.), Included in the list, usually lower down the pecking order, are things like mannerisms or a unique personal way of doing things. When you've been on stage for a while, you perceive that people begin to expect these, so you (unconsciously) begin to repeat them and then to emphasise them. Now, they may well have been instrumental in getting you on to the plinth – but they are not necessarily what's needed for the next phase. Indeed, they may sow the seeds of your downfall.

In my case, I had a reputation for being unpredictable – so I found myself searching the options available to me for one that would best match my reputation, and not one that would necessarily match one that was needed. Sometimes, predictable is good. I also had a reputation of being a hard-working, hard-playing rough diamond – so I worked harder, played harder and became more abrasive. I did that on occasions when the better route for me and the business would have been to work better, play softer and sandpaper myself down a bit. But King Billy BB rode again.

It took a while to recognise the symptoms and it took a while to repair the damage and shrink my testes down to some manageable size. Neither action may have been totally successful – but my message here is simple: A BBB state of mind creeps up on you without you noticing, even if you think you have defences in place. The long-term costs can outweigh the benefits of your fifteen minutes of fame.

I have one further message to pass on in this section: as I noted, our youngest son, Ben, is responsible for naming this dangerous adjunct to fame. It seems that the W Gene is alive and well for another generation.

23

We are family

The move to Florida brought profound changes to our family life. I would align them with the changes that the 2011 tsunami brought to the nuclear industry in north-east Japan.

To the outsider looking in, these changes were quite simple to quantify: as a family, we had won one of life's lotteries. It would be hard to stand at a debating lectern and argue otherwise – but I'll have a go.

As a 'Boomer' born in the immediate post-war years in the developed world, I am one of a blessed generation. My country has been involved in 'minor' wars, but has never been threatened in a way that it was before I was born, and I have never been threatened with being conscripted into the armed forces. We are living longer thanks to developments in healthcare and diet. We have been able to create more wealth on a wider scale than any previous (and maybe future) generation. Developments in travel, communication and household technology have made our everyday lives unrecognisable to those of our grandparents – and on top of all that, I get posted to sunny Florida on a chief executive's expat deal. A lottery win indeed.

Maxims are a popular fashion of today. Little cards or fridge magnets decorate most houses, and there is one that always catches my eye.

Behind every successful man
is an astonished woman.

I've known a few of the former, and – in fairness – they are often shadowed by the latter, but I would like to make my own contribution to the kitchen maxim industry:

Behind every successful expat married man are:
A wife who uses litres of super-glue to keep the act together
and
children who, on occasion, do not know
whether they are having a crap or a haircut.

I have referred previously in this opus to a famous, albeit anonymous and unheralded outside the county, Lancastrian poet. Buried in his life's work are some of the great pieces of modern imagery. Our default climate in the north-west of England is damp and cold, and everyone has a streaming nose from late October until Easter. It is true that the disappearance of the pea-souper fogs of my youth have eased the mortality rates, but nobody in the county has any doubt that long sleeves were invented so that the cuffs could be used to wipe tram- lines of snot away. Our poet hero captured this ever present symptom with the immortal line: 'His nose was running like a glassblower's arse'. Now, I have never seen one, nor do I want to – but if there is a finer piece of imagery in English literature, I have yet to read it.

On the modern desperation to be slim, his[26] body of work has another gem. Writing where the county flag has a pie hidden in it (just behind the red rose, if you look closely), and the default state of its citizens is 'big boned' – he cynically comments on those of unnatural slenderness as follows: 'I've seen more fat on a butcher's pencil.'[27]

It is to this genius I am going to turn to for help is trying to analyse just what happened – for better or worse – when the Head of Clan Gibbons was posted abroad. The bit I want is buried in one of his great works: ('If Sir Alex Ferguson is the answer, the question's shit'), and it comes in verse thirty-five, line six:

A parent can only be as happy
as the least happy child.

As a member of a blessed generation, who – by many definitions

---

26 Nobody knows if it is a him or a her. I am sure it is a him.
27 No, me neither. But you don't need to ask. Just let your imagination flow a bit…

– added to his fortunes by winning a 'lottery', I am not going to drift into the current British default mode of whingeing.[28] What I am going to say is that the events and experiences changed the trajectory of (all) our lives, and not all the variables were on the positive side of the balance sheet. As to the 'net, net' total – for the collective family and the individuals concerned – I simply don't know. Whether we benefitted – again, collectively or individually – in the long term is impossible to gauge, as you would have to employ the Harvard Qualifier[29] to the thesis – and none of us can begin to picture what might have been if this hadn't happened.

The key relationship, I suppose, was that between Judy and me. I have always admired Tom Waits' definition of the route to an effective relationship: 'When two people know the same things, one of them is not needed.' Judy and I agree that we have taken that to a new level, i.e.: 'When two people occupy the same *planet*, one of them is not needed.' It has been quite clear over our decades together that we are both needed as she clearly occupies a spot on Earth and I seem to occupy some (as yet undiscovered) planet in another galaxy. We only differ as to amount of time I spend on my Earth visits. I am quite happy to agree that I spent most of my time during this book away from Earth as far as the family were concerned, whereas Judy thinks I was actually born there and pop down only on rare occasions – these days to buy her an occasional Costa coffee, then on Thursdays as we look after our granddaughter and finally for our annual trip to Thailand.

There is no doubt that while I was at the helm of Burger King she was anchoring the family, handling the complexities and stresses of homes and families separated by nearly five thousand miles. As with a lot of expat situations, there was a lot of budget available, but not much support – and there's a big difference.

Let's marshal the facts. We knew around October 1988, as a family, that the move was definitely going to happen in January 1989. Judy and I had both parents alive and although their lives were not directly affected, both the idea and the practicalities of us living on the other side of the Atlantic needed a lot of thought and planning as far as they were concerned. We told them jointly at Christmas 1988 and, whereas they were excited for us, they were also a bit flattened by the implications.

28 Everybody whinges now – either from the Right (*Daily Mail*) or the left (*Guardian*).
29 The HQ is to say simply 'Compared to what?'

Both the boys (Ben, aged eleven, and Jon, aged fifteen at that stage) were day-attendees at a local private school – which although not a boarding school per se did have a small boarding facility. This facility was to figure significantly in our future plans. I have given enough views – directly and indirectly – on the British schooling system in Book One, so I'm not going to go off on an unstructured rant here. I have few material regrets in my life, but sending the boys to a day-attendance, fee-paying, school in England is one of them. We did it because we could (just) afford it, and we did it because we thought it would benefit them – and my regrets are not because the concept isn't right and doesn't work. I know a bundle of kids for whom it has worked just fine, and it seemed to be doing so for our two – it is just that, much later in life, my reflections are that it fails a Test of Rightness.

A plan emerged. I would head off on a solo mission in January, and Judy would stay back in England with life and schools as normal and manage the transition issues from that side of the pond. As soon as I could (amongst all the other stuff), I would get a handle on getting somewhere to live and finding schools – and when we had sorted all that out, we would complete the move. We had to make a decision on our home in England – did we keep it and use it occasionally, keep it and rent it out, or sell it?[30] Inasmuch as we could delegate the decisions to the boys, we did so – with Jon deciding to stay in England and move into the boarding facility and Ben solid in his determination to come with us and continue his schooling in Florida. Our Golden Retriever would come over during the transition, and stayed with me at our interim rented house.

The plan duly happened, and here is not the place for a detailed log of events. It is the place to highlight the difference between corporate budgets and support for families going through the expat experience. GrandMet threw money at the American end of this experience: they bought us a fine house and furnished it; they paid for private schooling for Ben; they were unquestioning and generous in their expenses associated with travel and transition – but their support for wives, floundering in the wake of all this upheaval, was simply non-existent.

Luckily, for the guys involved and for GrandMet, It turns out that Judy – and all the wives who came out with their British husbands to

---

30 We kept it. Judy issued a papal directive on the subject. It was one of the best decisions made.

join me in Burger King – had what I call Tenko characteristics. You may remember *Tenko* on the television: a series of expat British women somewhere in Asia in 1941, facing the threat and consequences of the Japanese invasion. There were a bundle of children needing rescuing, and a mountain range to get over. The Tenko women's approach was to whack one child under one arm, another one over the shoulder, pack a light cardigan in case it got a bit chilly above the snowline – and set off and get the job done. That's what won the day in Florida early in 1989. Of course, while they were all Tenko-ing away, keeping the domestic show on the road with duct tape and glue, we men were on our planets.

Now, here's the lottery-win bit: when it settled, of course it was an elite, fairly-tale life. I had a fat dollar salary, and rarely touched it. We had a house in which you could park an airship and a pool that could handle nuclear submarine manoeuvres. I got fat (performance-related) bonuses – the first one of which paid off the entire mortgage on our UK home. Friends and family from the UK came to visit and we could entertain them royally. We travelled all over the USA and the Caribbean, usually in style. We had membership of a fancy golf club paid for.

On the positive side, Ben and Jon put experiences in the bank that would simply not have been available to them had we all stayed in the UK. Ben scored a home run in Junior League baseball, and all but scored a touchdown in Junior Gridiron football. He was playing in the defensive safety position, made an interception and hared off towards a touchdown pursued by most of the opposing team. They got him just short of the line. In the half-time team talk, the coach praised Ben for his determined run, mistaking terror for determination. They both got to learn to play golf on a course where the fairways were like Axminster carpet and both of them hit the golf ball prodigious distances. On one occasion Jon did so, albeit after something interfered with his compass a bit. He stood on the tee and let fly. He missed the fairway; he missed the rough. He even missed the course's boundary fence. He put his ball right across *six lanes* of the US1 Highway and into a Ford dealership. Jon got his PADI scuba-diving qualification, along with me. I was under orders from Judy to 'look after him' while we were in the deep – a somewhat flawed request as he swam like a fish and would cheerfully stroke the whiskers of a Moray eel with a head the size of a football and teeth like Ken Dodd's. They both got as used to flying as if they were taking a bus, and usually turned left for their seats when they got on a plane. We used the corporate box at Joe Robbie Stadium in Miami for sports and entertainment – on one visit to see Guns N' Roses, Ben (then rising thirteen) spent much of the car journey there warning Judy that she would probably hear bad language.

And so on, and so on. Different experiences, certainly. Extravagant, daft, over the top, unreal, never to be forgotten – those too, on occasion. But the school solutions were running into problems.

From the outset, Ben did not like America generally, and the chosen American school particularly. In all honesty, on some days and despite what I owe it, his sentiments about America align with my own. It will come as no surprise to you that the Miami school was a top-end, day-attendance private school, and there was a disconnect with Ben from day one. He has inherited my dislike of ostentation and hated the peer group pressure at this kind of school to have the latest and flashiest of everything. Also – let's be honest – the W Gene made an occasional appearance in him, confirming its passage to the next generation. After less than two years, he made it clear he wanted to go back and board with his brother, who was then doing his 'A' Levels at the boarding facility of their old school. He moved back and our nest was empty – far earlier and with the fledglings a bloody sight further away than we would have anticipated. You can point to all the good stuff, but you can file that aspect under 'regret'.

You will have gathered that I am ambivalent about some of the great issues facing the planet – e.g. prostitution (see the King Billy BB chapter). I feel the same way about the great private school debate and its ancillary, the great boarding school debate. In a perfect world I guess there would be a need for neither, but it isn't, and they exist – and if they work for your situation, and supply meets demand without coercion, then the job's a good 'un as far as I am concerned.

I would make one point about boarding as a result of our experience. If it's right for your family situation, do it in a facility that's built for it and do it from the start. A genuine boarding school has processes, protocols and disciplines in place, often as the result of centuries of experience. If a kid goes in there from the outset, he or she grows up with it and that life becomes the norm. If you ask minors to do what we asked of our two – to go into that life in their teens – then you are asking them to face one of life's most difficult challenges: to adapt to a new normal. On top of that, the boarding facility that they went into wasn't a specialist boarding unit – it was really just a set of bedrooms on a day-attendance school. On top of that, the school was situated within walking distance of a busy, tempting city centre. On top of that, they were teenagers with strong early evidence that the W Gene had transitioned from father to son(s) – and you have a formula for a lot more going wrong than actually did.

While all this was going on, I was on Planet Gibbo – popping down to Earth now and again so that a queue of corporate folk could tug their forelocks in my direction, or so I could latch on to some outrageous family activity that would cost the equivalent of Darfur's GDP. I never saw it, but I know now that Judy used up yards of Duct tape and gallons of Araldite sticking and gluing as much of this together as possible.

So: bottom line. Did we suffer or benefit (collectively and individually) from this adventure? We – collectively and individually – did stuff beyond the imagination of most families, and there is the huge factor that we (and therefore our sons) are reasonably financially secure in a profoundly insecure world. On the other hand, we paid some prices.

After his disastrous decade, it was clear my father had cut off his rear-view mirrors. He simply never looked back, and never made value judgements on the past. I don't know whether I got my W Gene from him, but long ago I followed his steps and cut my own rear-view mirrors off. I don't really know whether, fully costed, we won or lost.

Don't know, don't care. We did it, but – just for the record – it wasn't all Guns N' Roses.

24
Winds of change

Have you ever felt that some unknown forces had combined together to get you at a certain place at a certain time for a purpose? No, I didn't think you had. Neither had I until August 1992.

Miami, along with most of the rest of the east coast of the USA, the Gulf of Mexico and almost all the Caribbean islands, lies in the broadest of broad paths of varying-strength storms and (occasionally) hurricanes from July to October each year. They usually form off the west coast of Africa, and – when they do gather strength and form a serious threat – their westward track is recorded and forecast nightly on US television.

In late August 2002, one such formation looked serious and, more to the point, looked to have south Florida in its sights. The USA National Hurricane Centre tracks about sixty or seventy of these each year, and while this one looked a bit nasty, in its early stages it seemed like just another one. On Friday 21 August it was business as usual for those in the Pink Palace. I was in London for meetings with GrandMet, and then flew to Madrid to meet Raphael Lavin, who was making great progress with our European business. The tropical storm – by then christened Andrew – was about a thousand miles off the east coast of America. When the business day ended, no one felt that their lives would be far different by Monday morning.

Like most responsible corporations, GrandMet had a Disaster Plan, and so did we in Burger King. Ours considered the effects of a fire, explosion, tornado or even a nuclear disaster from the local Turkey Point nuclear power plant that could contaminate all of south Florida – but it particularly emphasised the possible effects of a hurricane. The latter we planned would bring disruption for two to three weeks in the worst-case scenario, during which we would relocate Payroll, Accounting, MIS and Human Resources to back-up sites.

Saturday proved an ominous day as Andrew gathered speed and reached hurricane strength. By Saturday night it was clear that south Florida was a likely landing point but it was by no means certain, and nor was it certain – if the hurricane did make land there – where it would choose among the hundreds of miles of coast.

At midnight EST on Saturday (6 a.m. Madrid time) I was phoned with the news that the threat had moved from 'possible' to 'probable' and that the Disaster Plan was being triggered. I've had better wake-up calls, and my attempts to get a flight to Miami that day were fruitless. I went back to London as planned, and awaited developments.

Overnight, the position and likelihood worsened, and by mid-morning on Sunday an evacuation order was issued for properties east of US1 in all of Dade and Broward counties. The rest of the day echoed to noise of homes being 'prepared' and the fifteen members of the Burger King Building Services team doing what they could to do the same to the corporate buildings. The huge task facing them at the Pink Palace included shutting down everything (e.g. energy management, security systems, etc.), transferring emergency items to the inland Data Center and the removal of anything outside the building that could be turned into a missile.

Our Data Center – some three miles inland – had fire-rated interior walls and steel doors protecting its mainframe. It was seen as a super-secure place, with its shutters specially made for such an emergency. They took eight hours to install. The Technical Support team worked until midnight backing up the systems to record files. A bunch of evacuated families moved in for the duration.

In just a few hours, south Florida became a ghost town.

As Sunday night came, tens of thousands of people in south Florida holed themselves up in their 'safe rooms'[31] and tried to sleep. Children seemed to have been the most successful in this attempt.

At around 3.30 a.m., the third strongest hurricane to hit the US mainland for a century hit Dade County – with sustained winds of 145 miles

---

31 Every home was advised to so define one of its rooms – preferably the one with the least number of windows – and stock it with flashlights, candles, radios and (most importantly) mattresses which were more for protection than sleep.

per hour and gusts of up to 175 miles per hour mph. It hit the coast at a point on the bay between SW 164th street and SW 184th Street – the *precise* location of the Burger King World Headquarters Complex.

It is not the purpose of this book to detail the terror, destruction and acts of heroism that occurred over the next couple of hours. A hurricane has two prime damaging elements: first, the ability to pick up missiles (as big as trees or cars) and hurl them against anything or anybody in its path and, second, if it can penetrate a building – through a smashed window or broken roof – to create an internal vortex that simply destroys everything, including the roof.

The Pink Palace, in fairness right in the bull's eye of this monster, suffered dramatically from both.[32] Despite many acts of physical strength and plain bloody-minded heroism, the Data Center survived as a structure but was penetrated – and systems back-up was switched to Grand-Met sites in Minneapolis and Seattle. All the surrounding neighbourhoods were devastated and three hundred Burger King employees lost their homes completely, while all the rest suffered material damage.

The phones were down, but eventually news reached me back in London. It was when I got news of a list of employees that had been found *alive* that I began to realise the magnitude of what we faced. Even then, I did not know that we would be initiating a recovery effort so massive that few companies in the US had ever faced anything like it. Some companies have had their headquarters destroyed, some have helped their employees face personal disasters – but the destruction in Miami crossed all boundaries.

There were no flights into Miami, and no idea as to when they would resume. My frustration was immense, but then a strange development occurred. For some reason (I still don't understand) I couldn't phone into Miami, and they couldn't phone amongst themselves, but they could get an international line out – to me. My UK home became a clearing house for communication and information.

As word spread of the devastation, people began to emerge into the eerie new landscape on Monday morning. There was no power and no water supply. Phones were an unknown quantity, with no landlines and

32 Many people claim to have been the first to see the place on the morning after. No matter who was first – the impression was the same – the destruction was awesome. Dave Fitzjohn, another of my imported Limeys who headed up Real Estate (and who was to play a massive role in the future recovery) called it a minestrone: a 'huge vat of ceilings, wires, pipes, computers, furniture and paper'.

cell phones in overload. A curfew was imposed (7.00 p.m. to 7.00 a.m.) and the National Guard moved in to prevent lawlessness and looting.

As information dribbled into my clearing house, a single message became clear: on top of all this, people expected to lose their jobs as we would obviously take advantage of the situation to move the headquarters out of the Pink Palace and, indeed, out of Miami to Minneapolis. Every employee we reached had three simple questions: Will I have a job? Will the company rebuild? If so, will it be in Miami?

Away from the carnage, with the benefit of not being up to my armpits in snot and crocodiles, I realised I faced the biggest single decision of my business life. For sure, I was responsible for a brand that sold a million Whoppers a day, and made millions of dollars in profit – but this was something different. When I closed my eyes to think, I didn't see sandwiches or dollar bills, I saw families and faces. In all honesty, the decision wasn't that hard.

It became obvious I couldn't get back to Miami before Thursday 27 August, so I continued to use my UK base as a communications centre – and to do some fundamental decision-making. I talked directly with my US boss, and with Allen Sheppard. Their message was clear and consistent: say and do what you think is right – we will support you. You don't get many of them in a pound.

Through the laboured communication links, I was able to get a message out to our employees via the South Florida radio stations. I had made up my mind that we would rebuild and recover, and after taking a deep breath I taped the following message:

1. Don't go to the office. It is structurally sound, but badly damaged. We will salvage stuff in an orderly and systematic way – so you concentrate on stabilizing your domestic situation.

2. *As soon as possible* we will establish a physical and/or phone communications centre. KEEP LISTENING.

3. Business is going on. Systems have been transferred to a back-up site. YOU WILL BE PAID.

4. There will be obvious disruption. We will have to work from temporary accommodation and/or our homes – BUT THE INTENT IS TO GET BACK TO NORMAL, HOWEVER LONG IT TAKES.

It was not until quite a long time after that I understood the effect that this short message had. For many people it was like switching a pressure relief valve – they were still in a 'family'; despite there being no banks open and no ATMs, they were going to be paid[33] and so have some money to buy food and stuff; and somehow, sometime, they would have a job and place of work again.

My role in these books is to try and be the narrator – the guy (just) on stage when a set of circumstances and people come together. When I look back on this time, my mind is like a highlight reel – a series of short videos illustrating the weird and wonderful events that occurred in the immediate aftermath of this monster storm. Here are some:

- When I arrived back in Miami on the 27th, we established a Control Centre in the Function Room of a hotel twenty-five miles north of our Headquarters, which had not been anything like as badly affected. On the door was a yellow Post-It note, proudly bearing the handwritten words *Burger King Corporation: World Headquarters*.

- We established some marquees[34] and caravans on the Headquarter site. You queued up at one caravan for your payslip, and then went to another one for your pay – in cash. This bit was done under the watchful eye of a National Guardsman, armed with enough weaponry to equip a medium-sized Middle Eastern insurgency.

- The Blue Shirts arrived: twelve trained psychologists to provide counselling, at the company's cost, for anyone who needed it. Little used at first, this stayed on as an eventually much-used facility for nearly a year.

- One marquee provided essential services: food, water, ice, diapers and clothing.

- Kurt Romans, the company's Catering Services manager, took over one marquee (plus the Burger King Bus) as a kitchen and dining facility. For seven days a week, twelve hours a day, anybody who was hungry got fed.

- Within two or three days, two corporate wives heading a task force

---

33 Cash was like gold in the first couple of weeks – to buy generators, essentials, insurers' deposits, etc.

34 Actually these were bloody big circus tents, with a/c units. Courtesy of Coca Cola.

had secured, in Burger King's name, seventy house leases for those who simply had no home.

- The '7-11' task force drove upstate every day to get a supply of drugs and medicines for those who needed them. We had one baby with leukaemia and another with allergy that required a hard-to-get formula. These guys got hold of medications for both.

- Dave Fitzjohn, whose own house needed a six month rebuilding project, began the clean up and massive rebuilding of the Headquarters and Data Center. The Pink Palace once again triumphed in its planning myopia – it had been built in the worst possible spot for a recovery of this nature with a combination of heat, humidity and salt water.

- As cell phones came back on, we invented 'BK Radio'. Two freephone numbers were secured. On one of them you could ring in and tell us of your problems, and on the other you could dial in and listen to me, in my best Manchester accent, giving a daily status report and (the W Gene had been battered by the wind but was far from dead) some of my random thoughts. I deliberately kept this bit light and sometimes funny. It became such a success I kept it on – but on a weekly basis – way after all this stuff was over.

- A young Burger King couple who had a wedding planned in a church that was now rubble, and a reception planned in a hotel that was now looking like a bit of tired Yorkshire dry-stone walling, had them both provided in one of our marquees.

- By 7 September we had secured office space for a hundred people up by Miami Airport. We managed to fit three hundred in.

And so on, and so on. It was Mark McCormack, founder of the IMG agency, who wrote a book entitled *Things They Don't Teach You At Business School*. Our days (and nights) were made up of things that would never enter your head when you were putting a business plan or a budget together.

We decided on an early employee meeting, so that they could read our lips when we said we would rebuild. It was scheduled for the Big Tent on 2 September – and it was obvious way before we kicked off that we had a hell of a turn out. The opening had a bit of drama all of its own, albeit one unseen by most of the audience. We had still not traced everybody – and with fifteen minutes to go to kick off we still had not had confirmation about one female employee being alive and well. Finally – *finally* – we got a broken cell phone connection with her. She was OK, and had made it down to the Florida Keys with a relative.

From the outset, it was clear something had changed. It was no longer us and them. It was no longer GrandMet and Burger King. It was no longer Americans and Brits. It was not even senior management versus the rest. We were a united family taking this on. Of course, 'uniformity' of dress helped the unified spirit. Most people had only the clothes they were wearing when the hurricane struck – with the rest of their wardrobe being dumped by Hurricane Andrew somewhere in Texas.

When I started by telling them that we had JUST confirmed that everybody in and associated with the Burger king family had survived, and that we had no serious casualties and that we were – *as of right now* – starting our way back, they lifted the fucking roof off the tent. I'm sorry about swearing there. There are those who argue there are no suitable places for swearing. I disagree; it was for precisely times and places like this that swearing was invented. No other words would do it justice.

Two more tents were in use at that meeting: the first was what we christened the World's Biggest 7-11 – full of water, ice, canned food, clothing, medical supplies, baby formula, bandages, shampoo, toothbrushes and just about everything you could think of. But it was the other tent that made people's jaws drop. In Tent Two, there were a series of booths – a bit like a trade show. The booths included:

- A doctor for all medical questions.

- Representatives of the Company's 401K programme for immediate cash withdrawals.

- Insurance representatives from national homeowners' insurance companies.

- Federal assistance via FEMA.

- A Dade County Schools representative.

- Construction advisors.

- The Blue Shirts.

- Information on the housing leases we had secured.

The Pink Palace on its knees

- Financial advisors.

- Moving and storage companies.

- A Kids Day Out programme representative – we'd organised for parents to be given some relief by fixing to take kids to DisneyWorld.

- And the most popular of all? The Häagen Dazs booth – our sister GrandMet company shipped in about (it seemed) a million luxury ice creams. Boy, did they go quickly. I did some damage to them myself.

The mental and physical effort involved in getting that show on the road in just over a week was superhuman. Anybody who could do so chipped in and did so. I was simply a member of a team. I said 'yes' and 'no' occasionally – but mostly it was 'do what you think is right'. Judy and the Tenko Wives were towers of physical and mental strength, but it was not just the wives of senior management that got involved. Spouses of both sexes, from all ranks of management and staff, contributed if and when they could do. – and I achieved a goal I set myself: that few people actually believed what they saw on 2 September. In many cases we had to force people to take advantage; they simply did not believe what was on offer, and that it was free. We had to tell them: 'This is for you. Please take it.'

I learned a million lessons I'm probably never going to use again – but how about this one? Marjorie Dams, while we were putting together a shopping list of people's perceived needs in the first couple of days, drew on her experience as a nurse and social worker to foresee some needs that we captains of industry didn't. She put feminine products on the list as shock can often alter a woman's menstrual cycle. Her training also taught her that, in a disaster, people turn to each other for comfort – and so she put condoms on the list. We bought $300 worth. If my face had not been permanently fixed in a Tiger Woods 1000-yard stare by that time, I might have questioned it – but when Roger Thompson came back that night he reported that condoms were the first things we ran out of. There's a lesson for conventional business right there: if you have a problem, isn't it astonishing what happens if you get other people involved in the solution?

Remember, I'm the narrator here. I'm no hero in this story – my role in all these weird and wonderful activities was often just to walk about and get my shirt wet from people crying on it. But I did have another, parallel set of responsibilities. This disaster struck in south Florida – and Burger King traded all over the rest of the USA and (by then) in about forty five countries. We were within a month of the year end, and I had to bring home a £6.8 billion business, within GrandMet's overall results and within accepted accounting rules.

In the middle of this surreal world, I sat down with our Head of Finance, Scott Colabuono. A combination of Alamo-style bravery at our Data Center and effective back up sites meant that our systems were basic but useable – and he felt that if we concentrated on the 'must haves' and ignored the 'nice to haves' we could close the books on time. His team set up in the hotel, I remember one of his guys telling me that the sight of our temporary computers in the hotel suddenly displaying our general ledger was perhaps the greatest moment of his life. To this day I cannot help thinking about his poor wife.

It was to be more than a year before we were back in our (redesigned) headquarters, and it took the same sort of length of time for everybody to get their homes repaired, re-sited or rebuilt. But just over a month after this shit storm hit us, we closed our books at the (financial) year end, and they were signed off by the external auditors. The figures showed more success – we beat our Business Plan by twelve per cent – but there were two other results that emerged that didn't even make the fine print of the Annual Report. First, GrandMet and Burger King had passed a Test of Rightness in the eyes of its external audiences. The second one was personal: I had a feeling that the Forces That Be had combined to put me in this place at this time – but that I was now running on an empty tank.

25

And now the end is near

When I was shaping this chapter in my head I felt I would be writing about three separate forces that came together, and which resulted in the curtain coming down on this Cirque de Soleil part of my life – but, as I sit down at the keyboard I'm thinking that there might actually be more. I'll be as interested as anybody to see how it pans out.

My employment contract with GrandMet was a normal rolling one – with a 'notice period' for both sides. That is, of course, the most irrelevant and unused clause in all senior management contracts – if they want you out they simply shoot you with diamonds and get you out immediately. If you want to leave, the likelihood is that you have another job lined up, so they won't want you hanging about like a fart in a Volkswagen. You are usually out of the door on the same day you tell them.

It was understood by both parties, however, that my expat 'assignment' to the Burger King job would be for at least three years. When that time had elapsed, things were going so well that I drifted into a fourth year (1992) without (as I remember) even discussing any other option with anybody. As that year progressed, however, I began to have thoughts about 'what's next'. My feet were not yet itchy but I was forty-six, by now possessing a Green Card and holding a good hand of career cards. It is also a truism that the more senior you get in an organisation, the less (timely) options there are to move onwards and upward – and I wanted to avoid the dreaded 'Special Projects' office back in London while they figured out WTF to do with me. There was no crisis, and I hadn't even raised the subject formally with the GrandMet warlords, but Judy and I had talked about it in a fairly relaxed way.

Then Hurricane Andrew struck in the back half of my fourth year, and everything changed. I was so involved – we all were – and there was so much to do that the idea of leaving, of jumping ship, simply disappeared. I simply could not have looked at myself in my shaving mirror had I even thought about leaving the business, and a hefty bunch of its people, in this plight.

The recovery, however, got underway with great momentum: the business steadied and then carried on growing, the plans for rebuilding the Headquarters and the Data Center were signed off and work began, and the extensive (individual) home rebuilding and repair projects also started. It became clear that it would be about a year before all these would have reached a stage that could be defined as 'back to normal' – and the feeling began to grow in me that if I stayed for a fifth year and we got back to that stage, *and* chalked up another (fifth consecutive) year of business growth, it would be a good time to move on. Indeed, the more I thought about it, the more it seemed that it would be a bad idea if I didn't.

Over my corporate years it had become clear to me that I was not a creative genius, nor was I a maintenance and consolidation man. Apart from being thunderously lucky, I was (a taller) Tom Cruise in the Rain Man, and for me to stay on after all this would have seen the squarest of pegs struggling to fit in the roundest of holes.

That's one of the three forces. The second starts with an element of farce. After three years of growth we decided to pump up the feel-good factor and have a franchisee convention. What you do for one of these is hire an hangar-sized exhibition hall and hotel and fill it with supplier's (existing and potential) booths – at their expense. You then hire a couple of high-profile speakers and some heavy-hitting entertainment (sponsored by suppliers) and the franchisees pay for their own hotel rooms. Thus, if you plan it correctly, the whole circus is self-financing. As a by-product you get a high-profile splash in the franchising world, letting both existing and potential franchisees know that the brand is alive and kicking.

It was not really my kind of activity, and I kept my involvement to a minimum – in fact, Judy and I only flew back from Europe the day before it started. The venue was Orlando, Florida, and when we landed back in Miami I got an immediate connection up there. Judy went to our Miami house, from where she would travel up the next day. It was to be a big one, as we had secured one hell of a guest speaker to open the convention. General ('Stormin' Norman') Schwartzkopf had just retired from the US Army after his high-profile media-friendly leadership in the (first) Iraq war – and was about to join the speaker's circuit. After agreeing to sign cheque for him that would have funded NASA sending a team to Mars for a week or two, ours was to be his first speech – and there was a huge amount of attention, both from within our industry and from the general media.

The night before the Big Speech Day, Coca Cola supplied the Beach Boys for a concert after the opening evening banquet. I say the Beach Boys, but what I saw were two old geezers who looked like Compo and Cleggy out of *Last of the Summer Wine* fronting half a dozen dimly-lit, wonderful session musicians and singers. Hey – a brand is a brand.

Cometh the Big Day and Norman's imminent arrival, it was clear that the attendant arrangements were also going to be big league. He was to be accompanied by the top brass from the Washington Speakers Bureau, his speaking agents, and also by a hefty security detail. The key people were all equipped with walkie-talkies and we awaited the grand arrival. I was in the back of the hotel somewhere when my apparatus crackled into life, and I got the message that his limo was approaching. As I was to welcome him, I made my way to the front of the building which had been transformed into some sort of military zone, with a load of guys – all with short hair, sunglasses, chewing gum and suspicious looking bulges in their jackets where you presumed their Glocks were holstered – standing around. The all clear was given, and in steamed the biggest, blackest limousine you have ever seen, complete with blacked out windows, but surprisingly on its own. The tension was palpable as, accompanied by the king of the security men, I went towards the rear door. It opened slowly – *and out stepped my wife.*

Oh, happy day. I just wish it had been recorded on video, but that was before mobile phones had movie-camera facilities – and the moment was lost to history, although not to my memory. What had happened is that my beloved Sheilia had organised my wife's flight up to Orlando, and had arranged with the hotel to have her picked up at the airport. As she was the wife of the Chairman and CEO of the company who were holding the convention, they sent their biggest, baddest car to get her. Judy, who drove a Jeep day to day, thought it was a hoot. I didn't tell her that she nearly got shot out of surprise.

The sitcom hadn't finished yet, because about ten minutes later Norman arrived, *driving himself in an old Toyota pick-up*. All hell let loose; I'm not sure of all the details but I think two security guys shot themselves in the confusion. What's all this got to do with the second force? As head of the business that was having the convention I was on stage a lot, including topping and tailing the General. It was no big deal to me – remember I'm half Irish. The Irish, it seems to me, have two base talents: they can compose and sing dreary dirges at the same time, and they love a stage. As the dust settled on the Big Speech and my noisy links, one of the Washington Speakers Bureau folk quietly approached me and said that, if I ever was to consider leaving corporate life, they would be interested in representing me as a professional motivational speaker. It was a busy couple of days, but not busy enough for me to fail to register that little gem of an idea.

OK, force number three. It doesn't really have the comedic elements of number two, but it had impact. After two or three months of the post-hurricane life, it was clear, even to me, that I was running on empty. We had sowed a lot of business seeds outside the USA and they needed attention and watering, so I had to graft endless flights and time zone changes onto everything going on in Miami. The recovery programmes for the headquarters and its people threw up issue after issue, decision after decision. To add to the gaiety of it all I ruptured two discs in the back of my neck that needed complex surgery and a personal recovery schedule I was just not able to respect. We gradually got our Miami house back in shape, but on the domestic side of things there were some complexities emerging. Our parents were ageing and no longer able to come out to us and visit – indeed, my lovely father showed signs of getting ready to meet his Maker. Neither Jon nor Ben were really taking to boarding back in the UK like ducks to water. For one reason or another, we spent a lot of time in the air across the Atlantic.

On top of all that, much to Judy's delight, I timed my mid-life crisis – and it was a cracker. The W Gene came out from where it had been hiding during Hurricane Andrew, and waved at the crowds. As mid-life crises go, it resembled midnight on New Year's Eve on Sydney Harbour Bridge. In all honesty, it's my view that everybody, male and female, should have one as a rite of passage into the boring old fart you then become – but it's not over-helpful if you time it in the middle of a period of your life that appears to be a blend of Waterloo Station, the Somme and the Eton Wall Game. For the record, it's nothing like its description in most women's magazines, but it can be tiring – and tiring is just what I didn't need. Add all this up, and never before or since have I been so wiped out.

It got to the stage where I was (too) easily talked into having counselling – and that snapped me out of it, although not in a conventional way. If you remember, we had a team of 'Blue Shirts' – psychologists who were at the Headquarters site for a year to help people with their assorted traumas after the hurricane. On the basis of nothing ventured, nothing gained, I agreed to have a session with one of them, paid for by myself. On the day, we sat for about three quarters of an hour, with him occasionally prodding me with five-word prompts – and me spouting the most asinine endless bollocks in reply. At the end of it he told me that we must have some more ($1000) sessions, and that I had showed all the classic symptoms of someone *whose father had not been there for him*. I gazed at him with a mixture of admiration and horror – admiration for just trousering a grand for doing nothing and, second, for getting the bit he did do wholly wrong. The horror bit came from me realising that it had been me who had not been there for my father. That corrected a few things in my head, but it did not do much to alleviate the overall impact of force three – I was burnt out. End of.

I mentioned at the start of this chapter that there may have been a couple more factors at work. I think there were, but on a subconscious level. I have mentioned that my father had no rear-view mirrors. Understandably, after the decade he had in the 1940s, he never dwelt on the past. He never looked back, and never talked about it. I have, I think, something similar – a dislike of overstaying my welcome. I am a great fan of the American Constitution in that in less than a thousand words it articulates how to govern a country. One particularly prescient clause impresses me: the two-term limit for its presidents. If you compiled a list of the planet's bad news countries, you would find a lot of them have suffered at the hands of leaders, many of them eventual despots, who have clung onto power. If Margaret Thatcher had been limited to two terms, she could have – would have – gone down as a great reforming leader. As it was, she overstayed and lost the plot. I'm not sure if eight years is right for a business leader, or whether it's five or ten – but there comes a time when it's right for all parties that he/she exits stage left. Subconsciously, I believe I was beginning to feel that for me to stay beyond the five years would see my performance start to tail off.

I was also approaching chalking up a quarter century of corporate life – which is a quarter of a century of working for a boss. I had been phenomenally lucky in that most of them had been supportive mentors, but they were still bosses – and however much they delegated accountability and responsibility, they still channelled your activities and behaviour and you were still responsible to them, not to yourself. In hindsight, again subconsciously, I think I'd had enough and was keen to sail my own boat.

So, there were five forces, in total, coming together. It didn't happen on a Wednesday afternoon at 3.00 p.m., but early in my fifth year I decided to start to force the issue with GrandMet. I had already talked with Judy about what might happen – and the potential positives and negatives – of prodding this sleeping snake. Once again, I cannot remember what she said, but I'll never forget the look she gave me.

Those of you familiar with corporate life will know all about annual appraisals. They are part of any big company's management development process – and are taken seriously, although the actual interviews themselves are often quite funny. If you have never seen David Brent (Ricky Gervais) appraise his accountant in *The Office*, find it somewhere and enjoy it – it highlights the absurdity of what can happen if an appraisal goes slightly off course.

If you get to a very senior status, it's a process that often gets done away with – if you think about it, there's not a lot of point. But I used to insist with my USA boss that we had one each year. In fairness, every year I found something out about myself which helped me – and sometimes it was quite funny. He would occasionally say (what I assumed to be) nice things ('When I bang my finger on some managers' chests it goes right through. When I bang my finger on your chest, I hurt my finger'), and sometimes marked my card as to a perceived weakness ('All your geese are swans.'[35])

In the Spring of 1993, at such a requested appraisal interview, I sat opposite him and took a deep breath. I told him that I had agreed to come for three years, and by the end of this year I would have done five. It would be another year's growth, and we would be back to normal after the storm. It would, I ventured, be a good time for me to move to something else in GrandMet that offered me the same kind of challenge that Burger King had done five years ago.

---

35 Is this a criticism or a complement? I think the former, but I quite like geese.

Wow, did that short speech change the nature of the conversation. Very amicably, we terminated the interview right there, and agreed to meet a month later by which time he would have digested my thoughts and looked into the options for me and GrandMet. I couldn't have asked for a better response.

When we met again, it was in his palatial office in Minneapolis. There were three 'sitting' modules in it – a desk you could play hockey on, a settee and an antique table with matching chairs he used for small group meetings. All I can remember is that we kept changing positions, with both of us occupying all possible seating arrangements before we finished. It took a while, as I started off by holding my ground, and, as we progressed, took an even firmer grip on it. His (GrandMet's) position was that I should give it another (sixth) year as they had no one who could come in to Burger King and nothing suitable for me. Another year would enable them to address both on a more relaxed timescale. It stayed friendly, but the positions hardened – and we ended with a grim-faced agreement that I would leave Burger King at the end of my fifth year (about nine months hence) and that if they had nothing suitable to offer me, I could trigger my own severance. In the meantime we would immediately start a hyper-confidential search for my replacement.

At this stage, he was actually standing by the meeting table, next to a chart pad. He started scribbling something on it with a big felt-tip pen, and I was at an angle where I couldn't make it out. The more I craned my neck, the more it seemed just like a bunch of aimless squiggles. In the end I asked him what it was as he seemed so engrossed in it. 'That, Barry,' he replied, 'is a hat. Out of which I now have to produce a fucking rabbit.' That is high on the list of marriages of statements and occasions that I wish I had made.

I had not expected to be able (effectively) to trigger my own severance, which would be based on my dollar salary. I went home to Judy and told her that we might have won the lottery.

This time, I kept my confidentiality agreement. We had recruited a potential successor to me a few months before, albeit with a longer probation in mind. Nevertheless, a plan emerged that I was to work closely with him, and – if he stayed on track – we would appoint him a couple of days before I left. Otherwise it was lip-sealing time.

We finally got back in to our re-designed Headquarters at the end of 1993. Almost all the domestic issues had been addressed. The September (financial) year-end had passed with another growth recorded. We were now trading in fifty-five countries. American Airlines had given me a silver award for three million miles travelled. My last 'BK radio' message was sent to all company voice mails from a bed in the New Otani hotel in Tokyo, with me chatting into the phone lying on a bed in my shorts. We had finally made a sensible inroad into this complex market.

I called a meeting for all corporate staff in the new Headquarters facility. The Corporate PR team were briefed just before the meeting, and my successor appointed. I gave the Corporate Communications team a CD, and asked them to play track five when I gave the word.

By that time, I had been asked a few times if I was going to leave when we got back to normal. My answer was always that I would leave when the fat lady sang. A short time into my address to the assembled throng I nodded to the Communications team, and Vittoria de Los Angeles began to sing Bailero from *Songs of the Auvergne* over the speaker system. I explained that, while not exactly fat, Vittoria was big-boned and that was as near as I could get. She could certainly sing. I told them I was leaving, and that I would never forget them or the time we had been together. I didn't tell them why, because I was not too sure of the answer myself. I didn't tell them what I was going to do, because I hadn't a clue. I told them who my successor was, and then, like Elvis, left the building.

I left by the side door, quietly, leaving my successor and the PR teams of Burger King and GrandMet to handle the ripples. Not only did I leave Burger King on that day, I left GrandMet and I left corporate life (and bosses) behind forever. I felt sure-footed and confident about the future. Others – some of them friends and family – were surprised and a bit stunned. My Bank Manager thought the W Gene had taken over my body.

It was all over. As Chuck Berry sang, rather croakily, "'C'est la vie" said the old folks, it goes to show you never can tell'.

Book Three

Cancer, my arse

Suddenly, I need to change my colostomy bag. Now there's a sentence I never thought I'd write.

Melanie Reid, *Daily Telegraph* columnist, 13 April 2013

26

Ten days that shook a world

First, a word about the title. I am partly indebted to Ricky Tomlinson in his heroic role as a member of TV's *The Royle Family* for it. His frequent summing up of a statement by following it with an emphatic 'my arse' left no one in any doubt as to his feelings on the particular subject. It was partly incredulous and partly irritated – and I cannot think of a better way of describing my feelings towards the disease called cancer. The title also has a second relevance: it is (technically) exactly where it struck me. It is the year 2010.

I need to tippy-toe into this Book because I am on shaky ground. My clear and stated goal, from the start of this work, has been to act as a narrator, someone who happened to be present, on stage, when a particular match-up of people, circumstances and location took place. Earlier in Book Two, in a moment of weakness, I described all corporate value statements that are written up, stuck in expensive frames and hung in assorted company wash-rooms, cafeterias and corridors as – and I blush when I repeat it – as 'cosmic wank'. The bad news is that I feel, if anything, stronger about books based on, and some even called, *My Journey* – particularly if the author is a perma-tanned ex-politician or a potato-headed twenty-two-year-old footballer. The fact of the matter, however, is that this Book is less about circumstances, locations and a fascinating cast of people and more about me – and my mortal combat with an uncontrolled cell division in my fundamental orifice. I stand accused, therefore, of stooping to the same kind of self-serving bollocks as did those journeymen.

Mea Culpa. But there are two points to this third Book:

1. The first is undoubtedly and unashamedly self-serving. It is frequently said that, whatever your ideas about cancer, if you eventually get it, those ideas will change. Nothing prepares you for it – not just the disease itself, but the effects of trying to cure the disease. And it is not just the physical side of this experience; your mind stumbles into places where, frankly, minds would be better off not going. So this short book/long essay (delete as applicable) is cathartic – the simple act of articulating it may help me understand WTF happened to me, is happening to me and what awaits me around the next bend.

2. It's this second one that may have relevance for you. In June 2013, the (magnificent) Macmillan Cancer Support published a piece of research that upset a lot of people's breakfasts as the media javelined the results into the public domain. Their forecast, based on current trends, was that by the year 2020, *fifty per cent* of the UK's population could expect to get cancer in their lifetime. Now, you (the reader) and I (the writer) have a temporary relationship here – and if you have not had cancer then you might feel you are home and hosed because I have had it for the two of us. But when you go home tonight you might look across the table at a loved one, a person who is infinitely more important to you than I am, and who has also not had cancer. In which case the probability is emerging that one of you will have the nightmare experience of having the disease, and the other will have another nightmare experience – of watching. In the event that the Cancer Pigeon does crap on you, there are a couple of ideas coming up which are based on my experience that may – I stress may – help you kick a few of its doors in.[36]

I'll get on to the ten days that shook my world in a minute, but I need to put it in some sort of context.

I mentioned in Book One that I had my first swim in the River Styx immediately after they cut my umbilical cord. My mother passed away

36 When I mix a metaphor, I mix a metaphor.

when I was three, so the only objective witness statement we had for these events was my father. We have, therefore, divided everything by two – but it does seem to be the case that I was born very prematurely, weighing in below five pounds, and not expected to survive my first night. Overseeing this drama, in the deep recesses of Hope Hospital, Salford,[37] were two Irish nurses who, mindful of my imminent demise, decided I should die with a name – and therefore wrote Kevin Barry on my ankle label. Those of you with a working knowledge of Irish history will know that he was a hero of the Irish uprising who was thoughtfully executed by the British – thus giving him and a double handful of others martyr status and the 'uprising', which was all but stillborn, enough momentum to eventually win the day.

At this stage in the proceedings I gave an early illustration of my ability to push doors marked 'pull', and early evidence of presence of the W Gene, by surviving the night – and setting off to pursue my goal of putting on another couple of hundred pounds. When my father was re-admitted to the proceedings in the morning, he found he had a son who was alive and who was the proud possessor of the working title Kevin Barry. Now, bear in mind that, although he was born in Ireland, it was as the son of a British Army officer who was stationed in Limerick. Who knows; his father might even have been part of the Guard of Honour who prodded Kev up the gallows steps. He decided, therefore, not to run with the full name; the 'Kevin' was dropped, the 'Barry' was kept and I swam back to the safe bank of the River Styx.

For the next six decades my health – like that of many others – stayed in a loose 'corridor'. If the left hand wall of the corridor was a very healthy lifestyle and experience, and the right hand wall a very unhealthy lifestyle and experience, I stayed away from both. It is true that a long and mediocre amateur football career saw a cracked heel, two fractured ankles, nine broken toes (including four in one go) and a removed knee cartilage, and that the playground in my junior school, which was like the north face of the Eiger, only slightly steeper, saw a double fracture of my right arm – but, generally, I stayed fit and healthy. I visited the gym regularly and, although I was pushing two hundred pounds and a bit bulky (which got me an annual mild bollocking from my doctor), my regular medicals came and went without much flapping.

---

37 For those of you who don't know it, Salford is a quaint little fishing village at the inland end of the Manchester Ship Canal.

I never smoked and have never taken a recreational drug. I don't drink on my own, and rarely in between social sessions – but if I get my feet under the table at a dinner with friends I can cheerfully down a bottle of Malbec (and wash that down with a couple of thimbles of Grappa), with the only noticeable symptom being that I sound increasingly like a *Daily Mail* journalist as the evening progresses. I had one lot of major surgery in my life, sorting out a bad rupture of two discs at the top of my vertebrae – but, all in all, it was not a life of 'extremes' in anything to do with health. This means you don't expect anything extreme, and have no experience of dealing with it – if and when it arrives.

Approaching my sixty-fifth birthday, I had a slight alarm – with some blood specks appearing in my stools. Coincidentally, the NHS national screening programme for colon cancer caught up with me – and pronounced my samples 'all clear'. My GP studied this information carefully, and announce that I had IBS[38] and gave me some tablets. Here's lesson Number One: cancer is remarkably clever – it can hide from the prying eyes of a test specifically designed to spot it, and fool a GP.

As my birthday was approaching, I decided to have a private 5000-mile health service, and it was during this that the clock started ticking on the ten days. I'd done all the tests and was sitting having my tea and chocky bicky with the doctor (who was being nicely positive) when a nurse came in and said there was a *slight* presence of blood in my stool sample. I'd mentioned the NHS test and result, and the IBS diagnosis, but the wise doctor said that I 'might as well' have a colonoscopy as 'you've paid for it'. So I did, a couple of days later.

I don't know whether you remember the film where Ursula Andress is shrunk and enters a human tube system in a mini-mini-sort-of-submarine? Remembering that is the way I get through the deep joy of a colonoscopy experience, but – armed with my NHS clearance and my IBS diagnosis – I was quite relaxed as the doctor in charge of the submarine thingy sat me down and turned my life inside out and upside down.

'It's a mess down there,' were his quiet words. They would do a biopsy, but I was to see a consultant surgeon within forty-eight hours. There was no doubt in his mind that it was a cancerous tumour in a particularly (his words) 'nasty place'.

I know, in principle, what happened over the next ten days – but if it's details and objectivity you want you would need to get Judy to write

38 Irritable bowel syndrome.

it down. She shadowed me everywhere with a notebook – an exercise which proved to be rather useful as the information we had to digest over the next few days was extraordinary, and to make any sense of it was like trying to take a sip out of a fire hose.

I had no extreme response to the news. There was no great fit of anger, no blaming anybody. I certainly didn't blame the NHS or my GP[39] – they responded to, and diagnosed on the basis of, the information they had. There was no great self-pity. I don't think I was even numb. I do remember desperately trying to remember where I'd seen a quotation, which suddenly seemed rather apt. Then I remembered, and looked it up. It was Gustav Flaubert in 1872: 'All my life I have tried to live in an ivory tower, but a tide of shit is beating at its walls.'

On a more basic note, a saying came to mind that I had often used in speeches to business audiences: 'Remember, one day, every bubble meets a pin.'

The meeting with the consultant surgeon came and went. The diagnosis was confirmed and I was booked for surgery within days. There was also a more extended conversation about a colostomy, which had been mentioned in passing by the guy who did the colonoscopy. I hadn't paid much attention then as it was only a brief mention – and I had no idea what one was (there is also no one so deaf as he who wants to be). My surgeon-to-be explained, to my unfettered horror, the whole concept in much more detail, but left me with the intriguing idea that my colon might, *or might not*, be able to be rejoined a few weeks after the operation – but he wouldn't know whether that would be possible until he was in my abdomen up to his armpits. In the event that it was not going to be possible to rejoin it, I would be left with what Marks and Spencer's call a bag for life. He did, however, have a plan: in the intervening few days before I went under the knife I would see a nurse who specialised in these things, and she would explain everything and would measure me up and prep me for the surgery.

She was brilliant. I realise that for most of her professional life she would be dealing with traumatised people, and would therefore be good at it – but her calmness and objectivity in explaining the equipment and the process to me shifted about half my unwarranted fears in ten minutes, although I did ponder a while about her postscript remark

39 And I don't to this day. Their processes are well meaning and excellent, but simply fallible – remember that.

that men have a lot more trouble handling this idea than women. She finished the session by measuring all sorts of things around my lower abdomen (e.g. where I wore my belt) and then drew *two* diagrams on it. On the right (as you look down) which is where it would be attached if it was temporary, and on the left if it was to be permanent. As a result, most of my lower abdomen was covered in blue markings, and I went into surgery with it looking like David Beckham's arm.

I checked into hospital the following Sunday night. Our son Ben had raided the Manchester City online store, and I was (rather embarrassingly) equipped with MCFC pyjamas and slippers to face my ordeal. After a while, Judy and Ben had to clear off, and I was left in an eerily quiet hospital ward, going through the joyful process of 'evacuating' my bowels, when who should walk in but my consultant surgeon – who I had not expected to see until I was on his operating table at 6.00 a.m. the following morning.

Any thoughts that this was a social visit were soon gone, however, as he revealed the reason for him missing his Sunday supper at home was to get me to a) understand a series of probabilities as a result of what lay ahead and b) to legally release him from any liability if any of these probabilities came to pass. In all honesty, I wasn't paying much attention as he droned on – I wasn't going to refuse the operation at this stage and I just wished he'd get the fuck on with it. But item number six caught my attention: at my age (sixty-five), and level of fitness (OK), given the invasiveness and severity of the operation (both big), there was a fifteen per cent chance I would not wake up.

After what seemed like a week later, Monday morning 6.00 a.m. arrived. Into the theatre I went. I had the joy of somebody who had obviously trained under Eva Braun shave my pubes off, and a few minutes later I was asked to sit up and face the wall as they inserted an epidural in my back. This was to be my last conscious moment for about five hours, and I remember my last thoughts vividly: fifteen per cent translates into about a one in six and a half chance of something occurring. It was not beyond the bounds of possibility, therefore, that I would not be waking up. It was, therefore, possible that my last sight on earth would be a pissant boring wall, devoid of any of anything of interest.

27

Chemical Ali

For somewhere between four and five hours on the operating table I repeated my 'swimming in the River Styx' exercise, first attempted when I was a few minutes old. Once again, I saw a door marked 'pull' and pushed it in, and swam back to the living side of the river.

I came to in the ICU of the hospital, and remember nothing until Ben and Judy appeared at the foot of my bed – trying (and failing) to look positive and encouraging as they peered at the face of someone they only vaguely recognised.

Sometime after they left, with the effort normally associated with a heavily drugged Olympic weightlifter, I lifted the covering bed sheet and had a look down. At the time I didn't know or remember what I was looking for, and the sight that greeted was confused and concerning. It was a mass of dressings and tubes – and a colostomy bag. A tsunami of a memory wave hit me, and I digested the fact that it was on the left side of my abdomen. That was the side that meant it would not be able to be reconnected.

It's amazing how the human body, at its lowest, can somehow find resources and strengths to do extraordinary feats. Right there, right then, I began swearing under my breath, and kept it up, for about five minutes – without repeating myself. Hey-ho, a bag for life.

At the time (apparently) that was the least of my problems. Recovery was slow – with the first major step up coming after a couple of days. That involved the removal of my epidural tube from my back, a pain relief system known and loved by many new mothers. I was operated on at dawn on a Monday, and they took it out on Wednesday afternoon, under the misguided assumption that about five hundred paracetamol an hour would compensate. It was not enough, and the results confirmed that the hugely invasive surgery had not interfered with my W Gene. I was told that my recovery was on track, which is why they felt that they could change the pain management system – all very well for those who were changing it but, and you can take this from me, some distance away from a barrel of laughs for the victim of the change. As they fixed me up to go to sleep on Wednesday night, the lower half of my body felt as though it was being danced on by an elephant wearing stiletto heels that had been adapted as welding irons. About one hour into the night, up popped the W Gene. For some reason I decided to alleviate the pain by *making my bed* as it appeared a tad untidy. Not unreasonable, surely? Up I got to address the task, and immediately ran into two (what I will call) barriers. Number One was that I found that I could not stand. Number Two was that I had *five* tubes attached to, or inserted in, my body. I am sure of the exact number because I can remember the exact quote of the (otherwise delightfully sophisticated) nurse who sprinted to the rescue and who almost beat my recently established swearing-without-repetition record. In all fairness, it entertained the ICU for a bit.

I got home after a week. I wasn't ready – but in an astonishing discharge speech my consultant told me that I had a lower risk of infection at home than I did in the hospital's ICU. ICU, remember, stands for Intensive Care Unit. As the Yanks say, 'go figure'

After just over a week, I found that I had lost an astonishing eighteen pounds – but I set about my three tasks: a) managing my colostomy, b) recovery and c) preparing myself mentally and physically for chemotherapy. The latter, on the advice of my surgeon and (a newly arrived on the scene) oncologist would be delayed by about three to four months – their thoughts being that it would take this long to build me up to a level where they could then knock me down again.

But it was here, gentle reader, that the fickle finger of fate intervened with the first positive ingredient being chucked into this murky soup.

Before the Ten Days that shook the World, I had been planning a bit of a do to celebrate my sixty-fifth birthday. It wasn't about retiring – my position was similar to that of the veteran US golfer Lee Trevino who, when asked about possible retirement, replied 'I play golf and fish, what would I retire from?' I had been writing books and giving speeches for twenty years – but thought I might waft my cap at my sixty-fifth birthday to celebrate starting to pick up my UK (and US!) state pensions. The event was to be at the end of January in 2011, but as this lot hit me in the immediately preceding December, the first thought was to cancel or postpone it. It was my surgeon who intervened. In his view I would not be able to face chemo until at least March – and he felt the celebration, far from being a negative, might be (literally) just what the doctor ordered in terms of a mental and physical uplift before I became Chemical Ali.

The planned bash was to take our family to Thailand. Ben had recently been showing vague signs of becoming serious with a (simply delightful) lass called Katie, so both of them were invited to join Judy and I over there. Jon was in Bali, so he would join us from there. It was me more than anybody else who needed convincing but, after a lot of mulling it over, the trip was back on.

Just short of two months after the operation, I set out for Heathrow Airport armed with enough medical and surgical supplies to keep the Greek National Health service going for about a month.[40] I immediately stumbled over the second positive factor in all this. If you have a colostomy, you are given an International Travel Certificate (in about twenty languages) which enables you to demand a private room if Customs or Security ask to 'pat search' you. The reality is that once the average security officer sees the certificate, he or she goes grey-faced and waves you through. I haven't tested it but my theory is that, armed with my precious certificate, I could get through Luton Airport carrying a rocket launcher.

The trip came and went with a lot of joy and a few moments of stress. Judy had her boys together for the first time for a couple of years, and spent much of the trip wearing a smile (here's that Lancashire poet again) like a dog with a tin willy. As it turns out, a colostomy is no big (practical) deal. I was back in the gym and could wander around the beach in my usual M&S swim shorts. The issue with the colostomy is you must plan for it going wrong, but once you have done that it very rarely does if you watch your diet and eating patterns. By now, every day was bringing a new realisation that life could and would go on, and that there were positives in the air again. As it happens, fate decided to throw in a really big positive one – although we didn't realise the spoils until later. Our first grandchild was conceived, and would arrive in November – on the first anniversary of the start of the ten days that shook the world.

---

40 That is, one pretty full duffle bag.

When I got back, my 'honeymoon' was over, and I had to start chemotherapy. Deep Joy.

Cancer has been known and recognised as a disease for nearly 5000 years – with the first recorded reference being by an Egyptian doctor called Imhotep in 2625 BC. For the vast majority of its history the solution was either pray or undergo (increasingly) invasive surgery – until radiation and/or chemical therapy came along as a substitute or adjuvant approach. It will give you some idea of the unfettered gaiety and fun associated with chemotherapy if I tell you that the real breakthrough for this science came with the development of mustard gas in World War One – a product that killed and/or savagely damaged millions.

I'm going to chuck in the occasional 'lesson' as I go through this – not to provide any kind of 'ops manual', but just in case you (or somebody close to you) is faced with this experience. These are my observations – the first being that, if a doctor tells you that, for an upcoming procedure, you can have a general anaesthetic or a local anaesthetic, immediately plump for the general. Don't hesitate. Don't listen to anybody. Don't try and apply logic. Don't bugger around with Minimax Probability Theory or Risk Analysis, *go for the general*. Before they started chemo, I had to have an inlet port surgically inserted into my upper chest so that they could then just 'plug' the tube carrying the chemicals straight in. I was given the choice of anaesthetics. Enter stage right Billy Big Bollocks, who chose the local. You don't need to know anything else – just *you* choose the general.

Here's the second observation, in fact it's in two parts:

1.   IMHO the science of chemotherapy, as practised by modern oncologists, is to identify, at the outset, exactly how much they think you can stand (based on height, weight, fitness, mental strength, etc.) – and then to prescribe a mix of chemicals designed to take you to a hundred and ten per cent of that.

2.   Seriously qualified doctors and consultants are brilliant at diagnosing and/or operating on and/or prescribing a remedy for your illness. They have *no idea* about managing the after-effects of their actions. That is entirely left to nurses who often earn about a tenth as much as the doctors. On reflection, it's probably as well they don't get involved.

My chemo was a living example of both these observations. It was ironic that I never felt ill as a result of my disease – but, Jesus, did I feel ill as a result of the cure(s).

Every fourteen days for six months I, and a nurse who (brilliantly) dealt with me through the whole programme, went through a three-day ritual. Day 1 saw her take blood samples, and if my red and white 'numbers' were right we progressed to Day 2. On this day I started with a stationary two-hour injection into my port. When this was finished, out came that tube (which had been fed from a bottle hanging on a pole), and in went another one. The latter was attached, via about four feet of flexible tubing, to a plastic bottle about the size of a beer bottle inside of which was a vacuum-surrounded phial of poison. That phial took *forty-eight hours* to empty – during which time I carried the bottle around with me. It just fitted into the pocket of my jeans, thus giving rise to the obvious and hilarious remark from friends and family alike: 'Is that a chemo bottle in your pocket or are you just pleased to see me?'

You don't need details of the next six months as the chemical poisons did their work – basically destroying my immune system at the same time as they (hopefully) mopped up any cancer cells that hadn't made it into the waste bin of the operating theatre a few months previously. An enjoyable side-effect was that it became almost impossible to get food down me. You'll have heard this from other chemo victims so often that it's become a bit of a cliché, and there's no point in me trying to describe this state of affairs to those who have not experienced it. I've always enjoyed my food and if you had told me beforehand that I would face plate after plate of appetising food that Judy had gone to her wits end to create for me – day after day – and I simply could not face it, I would have told you that you were mad. In the end, Ben arrived with a bag of stuff that – if you mixed it with water and/or milk – created a 'drink' that had about 3000 calories in a pint glass. If I refused it, he told me, he was going to hit me with the bag.

In the end, one of my old (sister) companies came to some sort of rescue, and I survived the last month on Häagen Dazs ice cream. You can file that under 'helpful hints' or 'unusual adverts' in case you should ever need it.

Eventually, my oncologist called the programme to a halt – with eleven of the twelve scheduled infusions completed. The good news is that I had not lost my hair; my particular blend of two chemicals meaning that it just stopped growing for about two months. I was north of fifty pounds lighter than the day before the original surgery, and if you half closed your eyes and the lighting was right, bore a remarkable resemblance to Keith Richards.

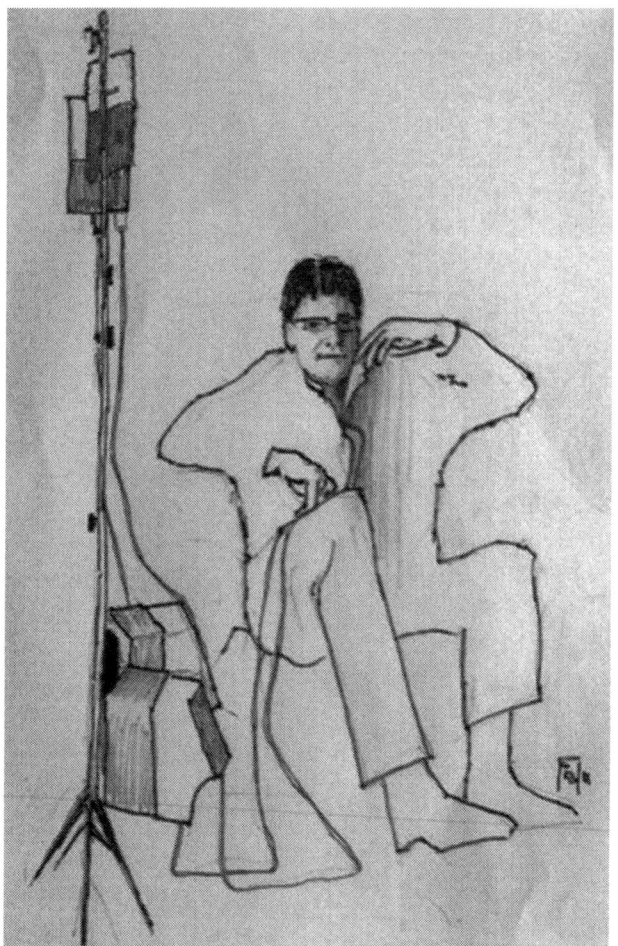

Self-portrait: the delights of chemotherapy. Note: the poison makes its way from the two hanging bags, via the tubes, into me via the metal port drilled into my chest. Deep joy.

The treatment – the combination of surgery and 'adjuvant' chemo-therapy – was over by September 2011. I had a CT scan and nervously arrived for the result. The doctor was sitting looking intently at his com-puter screen as we (Judy was still my shadow – I'm not daft) went in, his arms folded across his chest. He looked up and smiled. 'Hello Barry,' he said. 'How are you'? Honestly, that's what he said. I started to make the obvious reply, but Judy caught my eye and gave me The Look. The obvious reply being, of course: 'How about *you* telling *me* how I am'. I refrained.

I got the all clear. I'll be monitored now for five years, but I could now go about the business of rebuilding the lives of myself and my family. I had a bag for life to manage, and the chemo had left me with numb hands and feet,[41] something which looks as though it will be permanent. In November 2012, our granddaughter Holly celebrated her first birthday, and I celebrated the second anniversary of ten days that shook the world by convincing my (travel) insurance company to remove the cancer-related exclusions that they had insisted on for the previous twenty-four months. I did my first paid speech in front of an audience of five hundred at the Excel Centre in London, and afterwards wondered why I had been so nervous about standing in front of an audience for forty-five minutes with a colostomy bag that they couldn't see and didn't care about.

In the words of one of the great Moon/June poets of our time, Paul McCartney: *Ob-la-di, ob-la-da, life goes on, lala, how the life goes on ... .*

---

41 As a result of damaged nerve ends.

28

Death, where is thy sting?

If you are diagnosed with cancer in the UK, as in most developed countries, there is a load of help available. Some of it is technical and/or scientific – the surgeon removing the affected bit and/or the alchemic oncologist poisoning it (and everything else) and/or the radiologist blasting it – but a lot more help is available, not necessarily specific to you, from a host of other sources. It may be from people you know who have had the experience, it may be via the millions of words written about it, coming at the subject from all vantage points. There is, however, one source of help that must be brought into play if you are going to deal with challenge as effectively as possible with your own particular circumstances. That source is you.

About half way through my chemotherapy programme, I got a call from my GP's surgery asking me to call in. Apparently, my oncologist or surgeon had copied them in on one of the review notes after one of my visits and that had triggered the request. I duly turned up at the surgery and was ushered in to see my GP at the appointed time. It came as no real surprise that the left hand of this process had not conferred with the right and, after I sat down, he looked at me questioningly, probably expecting the usual runny nose. When I explained that it was his office that had requested that I come in to see him, and what this was presumably about, he uttered the immortal words 'Thank goodness for that, I thought you looked really ill'.

What followed was interesting. In his (and, presumably, the NHS's) view, an equal challenge to the physical one that I faced, in the immedi-

ate future, was the mental one. I would undoubtedly get stressed and depressed, and he wanted me to know that he would be there for me when
that happened. Fair enough – though remember that this was the guy
who diagnosed me with IBS. Him being there for me sounds about the
same as the Pope saying he'd be there for Judas. This diagnosis, though,
was dead right. The mental challenge is profound, and I've been patchy
at handling it. It's not that you feel depressed, or angry, or bitter – and
it's not necessarily at the start when you are first diagnosed and the dark
unknown is still ahead of you. It's more a feeling of being lost, and it
often hits you when the Big Treatment is behind you and everybody's
gone away and you are – metaphorically at least – alone.

I am indebted to Siddhartha Mukkerjee for his remarkable book on
the subject of cancer. He dug up a quote from a cancer victim. Her name
was Maggie Keswick Jencks, and in 1994 she wrote an essay entitled *A
View from the Front Line*. This is a short extract about what happens
to some people when they are experiencing the otherwise untroubled
airplane flight of life – and cancer strikes:

> There you are, the future patient, quietly progressing with other passen-
> gers toward a distant destination when, astonishingly (Why me?) a large
> hole opens in the floor next to you. People in white coats appear, help
> you into a parachute and – no time to think – out you go.
>
> You descend. You hit the ground ... but where is the enemy? What is the
> enemy? What is it up to? No road. No compass. No map. No training. Is
> there something you should know and don't?
>
> The white coats are far, far away, strapping others into their parachutes.
> Occasionally they wave but, even if you ask them, they don't know the
> answers. They are up there in the jumbo, involved with parachutes, not
> map making.

Quoted in *The Emperor of All Maladies*, **Siddhartha Mukkerjee,**
2011

I did not know Maggie Keswick Jencks, but I do know she is no longer with us, a victim of the disease she was writing about. What I also
know is that, as a description of the state of mind of a cancer victim, it

is centre-bull. I would, therefore, like to dedicate the next part(s) of this book to her memory. If you are going to beat the mental challenge of cancer (and what happens next) you need to create your own map with the roads ahead, and out of it, clearly marked – which from now on I am going to call the Jencks Map.

The first road out is dealing with the fact that your own mortality is suddenly facing you across the table. If it has your name on it, cancer is likely to strike in your later years – but, make no mistake, it can hit you in your infancy or in your dotage or at any point in between. From that moment on, your death is either certain, probable or possible. There's no fancying this thing up – it can be unbeatable. The cancer of Josephine Hart, Maurice Saatchi's wife, was diagnosed as 'malignant, advanced and inoperable' – which is up there with a judge putting on a black cap, sentencing you and then prodding you up the steps of the gallows. The good news is that it is more likely to be in the probable/possible range – but wherever you are on that spectrum, that's what you have to mentally deal with if you are to draw your first road on your map. If you don't, you stay in Jencks' wasteland.

Here's how I attempted it. I personalised the bastard – and I talk to him every day.

In my world he looks like Sir Alex Ferguson, with his face frozen in that look he had when an opposing team scored against United in (by his definition) illegal stoppage time at the end of a game. In a nod in the direction of the more traditional Grim Reaper, he is wearing a hoodie, and carrying a clipboard (which I will refer to later). I call him Sir Alex D'eath.

It is crucial that he never gets the better of me, and never will. When I get the final call through him, there will be no sense of victory for him. I achieve this by going to bed every night not being bothered if I don't wake up. Now then: let me repeat that for emphasis: I mean it – *it is no great victory for Sir Alex if I slide off this mortal coil at any time from now on in.*

There is a way of getting yourself in this frame of mind, but to achieve it there is a rule you must obey. This thinking, and these conversations with (your) Sir Alex, *must* be internalised – you cannot share these with your family. Philip Larkin's famous thoughts on poetry – 'Poetry is nobody's business but the poet's, and anybody else can fuck off ' – are right on for this approach if you substitute your conversations with Sir Alex for the word 'poetry', and yourself for 'the poet'. If people close to you get wind of this, they will frown and come out with patronising shit about you giving up when the opposite is true. I deal with my mortality this way, but I can still answer these questions as follows:

- Do I want to die? NO.

- Will I miss a bunch of family and friends if I die? YES.

- Aren't there things I still want to do? YES.

- Will I do everything I can to avoid dying? YES.

So what's the deal here? How can I reconcile these contrary positions? Is this emerging as one of the great mathematical conundrums of all time? Answer: no, it's not. The answer to the reconciliation is simple.

It would be easy to look at my life – with the business success, nice home, lifestyle, a bit of headroom on the balance sheet and a great family – and fall into the trap of labelling me what a Cockney might call a 'diamond geezer'. That is so much bollocks. For sure, like most people, I can do some things well, just as I can do some things badly, but what I have done is win five lotteries in the space of sixty-seven years on this planet. Now that's phenomenal – *phenomenally lucky*. Those lottery wins take the form of crossing the paths of five people, each of whom proved a game-changer in my life. The cast list is as follows:

1. My stepmother. She arrived in the lives of my father and me when I was five – like a sunrise after a particularly dark night for both of us. It is a mark of how she related to me that I cannot remember the word 'step' ever being used. She has been my mother and inspiration now for over sixty years.

2. Judy, my wife for nearly half a century. She has pushed me forward and pulled me back. She has whispered and shouted at me. She has despaired of me, and celebrated with me. She has anchored me and cut my guy ropes. She has made me what I am by being everything that I am not.

3. Professor Nelson (see Book One). Quite different from the first two in that I had about twenty words head to head with him in total. But those twenty words rebooted my life as effectively as any computer process of the same name.

4. A guy called Joe Parkinson. He's missing from this book insofar as he's mainly on stage between Books One and Two. A fantastic mind – and I mean fantastic. And a W Gene that was (and still is) just quite extraordinary. It's the size of a large melon, and is the envy of all of us who profess to have one of our own.

5. Allen Sheppard (now Lord Didgemere). Chairman and CEO of GrandMet in the late 1980s and early 1990s. Now, there *is* a diamond geezer – in fact, the defining one.

All five of the above have something in common. All of them, when they had options to do otherwise, chose to support and encourage me. As a result, there were five step-changes in my life. No, I am not a diamond geezer, but I am one lucky bugger.

Now you see where the reconciliation comes in. Now you see how I balance this stuff internally. Of course I want to do and see more; of course I would miss folks if I wasn't here; of course I will fight it. But five lottery wins is ridiculous, and if it comes tonight it comes – and I will go contentedly and quietly – so much so that I go to sleep at night quite genuinely with a smile just in case I don't wake up. That way, it will be *no victory* for Sir Alex, and he knows this. Every day he looks at me, and every day I see the frustration growing and his face getting (impossibly) redder.

But I've not finished yet. I may well be ready to go before he calls. I am so content with the balance of it all, if it starts going downhill, I might kick *his* door in, even if it is marked 'pull'. If my life becomes unpleasant for me and those close to me, and I have the mental and physical resources to do so, I'm coming – ready or not. The day I cannot manage my colostomy on my own, for example, will be the day I barge through Sir Alex's door. If we in the UK don't have our own Dignitas by then, and I don't have the wherewithal to get to Switzerland, I will create Lancashire's own Dignitas formulae. First, you fry up some Bury black pudding, gently, then crumble it. Then grind one hundred paracetamol tablets into a powder, and then make the powder into a paste with a bit of water. Combine the black pudding crumbs and paracetamol paste and spread thickly on a Lancashire oven-bottom muffin. Eat it quickly, accompanied by a full bottle of Bushmills[42].

---

42 A bit of advice here. If you are going to leave a note, it's best to compose it *before* the Bushmills bit. If you leave it until afterwards, you might come out with something that Willie Nelson might sing.

This whole idea is too much for Sir Alex to handle. He says nothing. He just chews his gum more frantically.

The plan was to finish his chapter with that squiggly sign – but I can't. I can feel a challenge coming at me, either from you or the person reading this over your shoulder on the bus. The challenge is this: if this is a treatise about coming to terms with your own mortality, where does this leave the millions – billions – of people who handle this (or who have it handled for them) via having a faith with a capital F? For many of those, their time on this planet is but a transition and, provided they follow their particular religion's operations manual, shortly after their last mortal breath they will be received by heaven's doorman, or find themselves up to their armpits in virgins, or even reincarnated as a butterfly or the blue bit in a wisteria. I realise I am reducing my audience (and potential fan base) by these billions, but the fact is that these are not available to me. If you can use one or more of these ideas to draw your own line(s) on your Jencks Map, I wish you good luck, and in the words of Dave Allen: 'May your God go with you'.

It's not that I believe it all ends with that last breath, however, and here's where I pull my final trick on Sir Alex. I told you my vision of him included a clipboard. That's because it is his job to handle the exit interview. The idea, put in place by the powers that be (in whatever shape or form they take), is to seek a programme of constant Japanese-business-style small improvements for the Planet, so you are asked to list your own Ten Things That Went Well on earth while you were present, and then Ten of the Opposite. Here's where I'm ahead of the game: I'm ready. I carry my lists with me, and here they are as evidence:

Ten things the Earth got right

1. Lenses.

2. Angkor Wat.

3. Pembrokeshire Coastal Path.

4. All poets (and some writers).

5. Charities.

6. Clean water to your house, and sewage taken away.

7. A beer when you have walked the Samaria Gorge in Crete.

8. *Private Eye* magazine.

9. Dry stone walling.

10. Mushy peas (soaked overnight).

Ten things the Earth got wrong:

1 The *Daily Mail.*

2. Space exploration.

3. Phone-in radio.

4. Mosquitoes and cobras (what *is* the point?).

5. Piers Morgan (ditto).

6. Chewing gum on pavements.

7. Televised darts.

8. Airports (immigration, emigration, customs, luggage, security, delays, overpricing and lies).

9. All religions apart from Buddhism.

10. Political 'initiatives'.

Now, there's my big finish. Sir Alex can see my pre-printed cards, and he *knows*. He is already on the back foot, and this is just too much. I have the first road drawn on my Jencks Map. He is beaten, and he knows it. He splutters and keeps looking at his watch – and finally his face reaches the state it did when Manchester City nicked the title off his United in the ninety-fourth minute of the last game of the season in 2012. That is, his face looks like a smacked arse.

29

Brave new world

Right. You've come to terms with your own Sir Alex D'eath: your own mortality. That's a clear road on the Jencks Map out of your wasteland. That's the big one sorted, right? Wrong – there's a bigger one.

One of Lewis Carroll's jewels was 'If you don't know where you are going, any road will get you there'. That applies here. It's no good having a road identified unless you have a place to go equally clear in your mind.

If you have been in a big organisation, and reached even a middle level of responsibility, you will probably have had the experience of 'letting someone go'. That's a modern-day euphemism for firing somebody or making them redundant or 'mutually' agreeing that they should leave the organisation. There is a key stage in the first phase of this process that you must achieve, otherwise there is little point in getting into the second phase – and that is that the receiver of the (usually) bad news understands and accepts the fact that it is over. There is no point in getting into what happens next – compensation, support, help etc. – until that conversation can take place without his or her mind still holding on to the thought that it still may not happen. There is, in their mind, a possibility that normal service can and will be resumed as soon as possible.

There is a similar principle in plotting a route on your Jencks Map. The road you want to draw on it must lead you to a place called the New Normal. This is a state of mind that understands and accepts the fact that something has changed *irrevocably* – and that what was your normal life before has gone forever.

You need to be brutal in defining the new normal. Consider the following two lists.

Good news new normals?

- You fall in love. Maybe get married.
- You win the lottery.
- You get a new job or a big promotion.
- You inherit a lot of money.
- You recover from a bad disease.

Bad news new normals?

- You lose your job.
- You end a relationship/marriage.
- You lose your home.
- You break both legs, both arms and six ribs in a car crash.

You will notice I put question marks against the sub-headings. IMHO all of the above will bring profound changes in your life – for good and bad reasons – but they are not irrevocable changes. However remote the possibility (e.g. of your partner ever having you back) it is not *impossible* that the old normal can return. In which case you are not in the land of the new normal and have, therefore, no absolute need to understand and accept it. I can only think of three sets of circumstances that demand such an acceptance:

1. Somebody really close to you dies.

2. You, or somebody close to you, suffers an illness, the results of which are life changing and *will not improve*.

3. You become a parent.

In the words of my much quoted Lancashire poet, in these cases once the toothpaste is out of the tube, you can't get it back in. In all three cases, there is no point in wishing and hoping that, one day, you will wake up and find out that 'it' never happened. There is a new normal to get used to – and, unless you understand and accept that, it's like the firing process: you will be doomed to wandering about in the wasteland of the first phase.

My new normal was *not* my cancer. At this stage my results show that the cancer exited my body via the surgeon's knife and the oncologist's test-tubes – and that my old normal could return if that was the full story. My new normal is a result of the treatment(s) I was given for the disease:

- As a result of the surgery, at least once, and sometimes four or five times a day, wherever I am and with timing over which I have no control, I have to deal with an open wound in my abdomen. It requires surgical cleanliness, bloody good eyesight and not a little dexterity. I will have to do it every day for the rest of my life. Now then: the actual management of that is not the problem – it's the planning for it that is burdensome. If I want to fly somewhere for a fortnight's holiday, I have to take colostomy bags and surgical supplies with me in my carry on – I dare not risk losing them with baggage I have checked into the aircraft hold. Every day, in every place, I have to carry spare supplies with me. Every day I have to plan on it going wrong – the good news being that it very rarely does.

- The aggressive chemotherapy has left me with damaged nerve ends; peripheral neuropathy is its technical name. The symptoms are numbness and tingling in my hands, lower legs and feet. I've already adapted to it – at first I couldn't fasten shirt buttons or tie shoe laces and when I tried my first outside jog I went arse over tit twice in my first five hundred metres.

I'm two-and-a-half years into dealing with these fundamentals of my new normal, and I have got better and better at the physical and mental challenges involved. Today, if you ran a CCTV camera on me for twenty-four hours, you really wouldn't know that there was anything different about the way I manage my day-to-day life – apart from some odd idiosyncrasies that would fall within the normal pattern of most people who do a couple of things in an odd way. In the new normal I can read and I can write. I can smell, touch and feel – albeit with the latter two operating from a new base level. I can do my gym routine and run five kilometres in (just) under thirty minutes. I can ride my bike and swim. My neuropathy does not seem to have diminished my ability to grip my Big Bertha driver and despatch a golf ball, over extra cover, into the next post code. For sure, there is the possibility that my late life ambition to be a flamenco guitarist, one on a par with Manitas de Plata, is looking distinctly iffy, but in that respect the new normal is no different from the old (see Book One).

And that is the good news. If you define, understand, accept and adapt to the new normal, an amazing thing happens. It's like rebooting your computer. It's like, as the Americans would say: 'starting over'. The new normal is, literally, that. You don't think about the old normal. You are not angry or bitter. Of course you have days when you whinge a bit – but remember the old normal? You weren't the handsomest guy at the dance, you weren't the prettiest girl in the class. You couldn't run a hundred metres in under ten seconds. You were often a bit short of cash. But your lot was your lot and you got on with it. Sometimes you had a whinge, but most times you didn't think about it. Welcome to your new normal. If, if, *if* you can get your head in that place, it is far more important than coming to terms with your own mortality.

The wonderful folks at Macmillan are on record as saying the biggest upcoming cancer challenge will be the management of the road out of it – or, in my words, the Jencks Map. In my experience they are so right. If you can back your own Sir Alex into a corner where he knows he can't beat you, and you can adapt to your new normal in the way you did with your old one – i.e., rarely even thinking about it – you have made massive progress in pursuit of your victory.

30
The X-factor

You are not out of the woods yet for the simple reason that the barren wasteland on the Jencks Map is vast and littered with still more mental and physical obstacles – and you have still more to contribute in finding a pathway out.

We are all a mixture of behavioural and attitudinal pluses and minuses. We are good at some things, and crap at others, and it is vital in this process that you are objective and honest enough to analyse your own wheat and chaff, and get the wheat working for you. In that way, you bring your own X-factor into the fight – which you can add to the work of the surgeons, radiologists and oncologists.

There's a gender variable to consider here though – I don't think the male of the species finds this easy to do. For sure, your average guy – in public – can do confidence (and, frequently, arrogance), just as he can do self-depreciation (and, not-so-frequently, humility) – but, let's face it, most guys are actors for most of their waking hours. In the privacy of their own shaving mirror, however, most of that disappears into a jumble of insecurities and loose, unconnected wires.

The challenge here is simple: to try and analyse what you are good at, and bring it into play in your battle. The opposite also applies: understand what you do badly, and try and keep that off stage. Both these are difficult to figure out on your own as your results are almost certain to be distorted – and it is helpful if you can gather input from outside sources. Parents and close friends of the same gender are useless as sources here (probably worse than you), but siblings and spouses can provide vital input.

There is, of course, another source of external input – particularly available to those who have been involved in an organisation of any size. I refer, of course, to the annual fire dance of your formal 'appraisal'. Remember, this is where you sit down with your subordinate (or are made to sit down by your superior) and for (about) forty hugely mutually uncomfortable minutes, the senior tells the junior what they have done well, and what – they never use the words 'fail' or 'badly' nowadays – are their 'areas for development'. This process, surely, could provide some sort of objective external input into this search for your own excellence.

I began to trawl my memory for some appropriate content from those I had experienced during nearly a quarter century of corporate life. That must mean I had at least twenty-five of these, but – try as I might – I could only remember two. I decided to give both of them a forensic analysis to see if there was anything revealed about my psyche and/or behavioural patterns in them that I could use in my fight against these unwanted cells in my fundamental orifice.

The first one took place in about 1973. I had rejoined Shell as a Graduate Entry (note the capital G and E) and had been transferred to their Head Office in London. The world was at my feet, and didn't I know it. If the word 'obnoxious' hadn't been invented by then, you could have had a couple of pints with me in the Shell bar and it would have sprung to your mind on the way out. They (Shell) wisely put me under the tutelage of a wizened old Scot, and – after a year or so – up came the appraisal interview. His name was Bill Crumless, and he was approaching his sell-by date after a fairly office-bound career. I had years of glory just around the next corner (or so I thought), and approached the session having done absolutely none of the requisite pre-work or pre-thinking. The old boy sussed me out in a second, and opened the batting with a long, *long* pause, and then opened with a strange gambit. He told me that he was 'only going to appraise seventy-five per cent of me'. In fairness, that woke me up from my state of insulting, semi-comatose boredom, and I began to listen and take interest. What followed has stayed with me ever since.

His premise was this: there was twenty-five per cent of me that he was not going to go near, so he would concentrate on the rest. The reason he was not going near that twenty-five per cent was that it was '*dark*' (his word). It was unpredictable, off-piste and non-linear. All my worst stuff came out of that twenty-five per cent – but (and here's the jackpot) *so did all my best*. He finished on the back of some of the most powerful eye-contact I can ever remember – and told me never, ever, to be afraid to reach into that twenty-five per cent, and that more good would come out of it than bad. I have kept faith in his advice, and it has worked for me – although I think the good/bad score is a bit closer than he might have anticipated.

I have remembered those words ever since – and I think the advice is more and more relevant to everybody as the years (and generations) go by. My belief is that everybody has a similar percentage in principle – although the actual number may be as low at ten per cent or as high as ninety per cent or anywhere in between, but one of the despairing things I see about modern life is an increasing fear to reach into it. In corporate life, I see, increasingly, that decisions are being taken by software or lawyers. If you are faced with a decision, it is easy to model the 'what-if' variables on a laptop and come up with fifty options. You then apply some probability theory to them and, bingo, the 'best' option is lying in your printer tray. Another route is to give your six possible/preferred options to your lawyer, and he or she will tell you the five you mustn't do – bingo, there's your decision, made for you, again.

A couple of years ago, I was invited back to Liverpool University, to address the MBA programme students. Surprise Number One was that ninety per cent of them were Asian Indian, although – with hindsight – I don't know why I was surprised. Surprise Number Two was that I decided to include this idea in my speech (for the first time ever). Surprise Number Three was that I spent over an hour on this subject, and this subject alone, with them at the post-speech question time. They were fascinated. They were young and bright, with their lives – business and private – largely ahead of them, and they were worried about the demise of the *individual mind* in modern life. Can it still have a role in a world of regulation, political correctness, the chip and the Web and a billion lawyers? My position – that it can and should – gave them a bit of hope where, worryingly, their position was that all hope was lost.

OK, External Input Number One says I have a part of me that's non-linear and a bit dark and unpredictable. Number Two is less complicated, but also a bit puzzling. I didn't have formal appraisals with Allen Sheppard in GrandMet because that was the job of my direct boss, who was (hierarchically) between the two of us. But we had many, many talks during my time at the helm of Burger King – some of them one on one. I had a period of intense frustration when I was under pressure to inflate our (already good) short-term profitability to cover another part of GrandMet that had put the ball in the rough. In Burger King we could, unfortunately, always do that by selling a profitable group of company-owned and run restaurants to franchisees – and we could credit the book profit on the sale immediately. The fact that it was *not* the right decision for the business and that it *eroded* the next year's profitability got lost in the panicky need to bring home the (collective) Group's full year forecast. All that's by the by, but it explains why I was sitting in Allen's office one day having the nearest thing I ever had to a row with him. As a by-product, I got a mini appraisal. In a moment of real frustration, I raised my voice a fraction of a decibel and enquired, ever so politely, why the fuck[43] he had put me in charge of Burger King in the first place. The famed twinkle in his eyes never dulled for even a nanosecond, and his reply centred around one word. I was, he said, the most *restless* guy he had ever met, and that was precisely what Burger King had needed. I spend a few minutes tidily tucking my tail between my legs and then went back to Florida to sell my restaurants, never to forget that word. Allen was as good a judge of human horseflesh as I have ever met – but if you had armed me with a combined thesaurus and dictionary I would never have come up with that word in a self-description.

So: some version of a *non-linear mind* and *restless*. That's all I could come up with after a relentless trawl of my externally perceived strengths. But I do value the views of the two guys that gave them, and I can see (now) how they have worked for me. The irony is that if you flipped both coins – i.e. took a more linear approach to life and a calmer approach to the pace of it – then both of those could be also seen as strengths. Indeed, you may see them as being (among) yours, and therein lies the magic of these X-factors. They *are* yours, and yours alone. I can see how, consciously or unconsciously, I have played them so far in this weird scrap against this monstrous disease. The non-linear thing is just a fancy, more technical, alternative, definition of the W Gene, and approximately twenty-five per cent of the time, I do ignore the received wisdom as to what I should do (or think) next and follow my instincts. And I simply will not allow the words 'repeat' and 'fade' to figure on my activity radar. And I am restless. That might be because I recognise that my mortality is in question and I need to cram in some things on my bucket list, or it may be that if I can keep doing stuff at pace – which

---

43 I should also point out here that this act of monstrous courage and insubordination took place when I was already a bit demob happy. The more astute of you will have noticed there was no such approach when Allen was interviewing me FOR the job.

keeps me mentally and physically on the front foot – I can keep the disease itself on the back foot and retreating.

They were the results of my search for external, objective, perceptions of qualities I had that I might use in my fight. My inner trawl did reveal one characteristic that I believe can also work for me, although the risk factors and the potential downsides are higher. I left Manchester almost half a century ago, but it is a truism to say that you can take the boy out of Manchester, but you cannot take Manchester out of the boy. Nestling somewhere inside my body, probably adjacent to (and surely influencing) my W Gene, is my Manchester 'sense' of humour. I highlight the word 'sense' deliberately, as it is not an ever-present quality.

Manchester humour is not better or worse than any other. Liverpudlians, Cockneys, Dubliners, New Yorkers and folk from pretty much everywhere else I have known can have their own slant on what's funny and how to articulate it. None of them are better or worse than any other – but they are all different. Manchester's is *extremely* different and, even within that position on the boundary, mine pushes right against the ropes at times. I do not need any external analyser to tell me that.

Some of Manchester's social climate was covered in Book One. De Tocqueville savagely summed up the dark satanic qualities of Manchester in its Industrial Revolution/Cottonopolis days, and if he visited today I think he would still find the legacy of that in what is now a reinvented, forward-looking city. Our humour is a complex mixture of – on the surface – negative components: sarcasm, cynicism, blackness and piss-taking. But when you mix it together it can be – that's *can* be, mark you – unbearably funny. The purveyor of such humour must have one characteristic – he or she must be able to take it as well as give it out.

There is not an iota of doubt in my mind that you can use humour as an X-factor in your own battle here. That can be your own, or that of your friends and family. It can be Mancunian, or your own geographical version. It can be a 24/7 onslaught, or a card played occasionally – but it is likely to be somewhere between the two for best effect. To state the blindingly obvious, it has maximum effect if it is played when you are at your lowest.

There are two occasions where my ability to laugh at the weird – in both cases provided by other people, but at my expense – helped me get up the other side of a Slough of Despond, and in both cases kept me up on (relatively) high ground ever since. When I got back from surgery – which was no more than a couple of weeks after the first alarm bells disturbed my otherwise quiet life – it was all suddenly sinking in and I hit a real downer. Joe Parkinson, the crossing of whose path is one of my lottery wins of life, on hearing the technical exactitude of the location of my tumour, chuckled down the phone 'That's what you get from talking through your arse for fifty years'. I laughed till it hurt – which was not very long. But I have laughed long, and sometimes aloud, at it many times since.

The second also had a lasting, positive, effect. I was bemoaning my luck at the bag for life one day, and happened to remark to a pal of mine that, in the full length bathroom mirror, I looked like a 'fucking Hoover'. The next day his lovely wife Margaret, from her position firmly towards the top of my friends-and-family-that-I-can-remember list, rang Judy and asked 'How's Dyson this morning?' Brilliant. Wonderfully, breath-takingly brilliant. My bag had a name. It is now universally known as my Dyson, and I can't help smiling (for God's sake – *smiling*) when I deal with it. The only drawback is that it sometimes confuses the guy on the phone when I reorder supplies – but my message is that the mental uplift from finding even the tiniest, daftest thing to smile about is worth a thousand pills.

If you have this battle on, don't underestimate the power of your own X-factors in helping you win it. It won't replace the surgeon, radiologist or oncologist – but it can add profoundly to the effectiveness of their work. Add it all up, and your ability to find your way around – and eventually out of – Maggie Keswick Jencks' map increases significantly.

31

Un-trivial pursuit

The American Constitution, drawn up by the Founding Fathers, reflects an astonishingly prescient piece of thinking. It's had a handful of amendments, but essentially has stood the test of time as the charter for the governance of a great nation. In comparison, the (almost) infinite European Union (assorted) treaties, rulings and missives, which actually govern no nation, are a staggering shoal of bureaucratic, misguided, administrative plankton.

There is one aspect of the American Constitution that has some relevance in the fight against cancer. We lived there for twelve years, and I was always fascinated by the phrase 'the pursuit of happiness' which is ingrained in the original document. You will note that it is the *pursuit*, not actually the state of *being* happy. In my early clever-dick days I pointed that out to some American friends, but they all looked at me strangely – so I gave it up.

The relevance here is that – sorry about this – all of us have cancer cells in our bodies, but not everyone develops cancer. The challenge, therefore, for everyone, is the *pursuit* of a cancer-free state, because technically you can never attain it. Obviously, if cancer does develop and you are diagnosed with it, that pursuit takes on a step-function increase in urgency – and the heavy hitters (surgeons, radiologists and oncologists) are brought in to provide invaluable, essential help.

There are, however, many schools of thought that feel that the pursuit, whether it be a proactive prevention or a reactive address, can be helped by lifestyle choices. If you live in poverty and/or in the undeveloped world, these choices may not be available to you – but the chances are, if you are reading this book, many of them are.

There are dozens of books or theses on this subject,[44] and I have read most of them (as you do in my circumstances). Despite the fact I was desperately searching for good news and ideas that might work for me, I went into the exercise on a platform of deep, deep, cynicism. My faith was in proven facts and science, but the more I got into it, it seemed, the more questions were raised.

The median survival times of those diagnosed with specific cancers follow normal mathematical distribution curves – but at either end of the curves there are oddities that are simply unexplainable by science. Some people die when they shouldn't but (of much more interest to me) some survive against all scientific logic and odds. I started to pay attention.

If you are interested, walk into a large bookshop and you will find half an acre of books on this subject, but this is about what nudged my attention and caused a change in thinking and some changes in lifestyle.

Cancer cells are, essentially, immortal. They need little encouragement to grow and form a tumour. Once that happens, you need to call in the heavy hitters (above) but whether you are trying to prevent that, or help them respond to it, there are things you can do within the choices you make in day to day life. They all revolve around addressing cancer's two prime weaknesses: a) when your immune system fights back against the disease and b) when your body won't create the inflammation on which it thrives. As the TV meerkat says, 'Simples'.

There are valid studies that indicate that there are lifestyle choices that can strengthen the immune system. For sure, some of them seem to be pronouncements from the Institute of the Bleedin' Obvious, but there are just too many supportive case histories to ignore them completely. Our immune systems are strongest when our diets are healthy (fewer processed and refined foods; more Mediterranean, Indian and Asian cuisines); when our environment is clean (less cigarette smoke, fewer environmental and domestic pollutants) and includes more physical activity that involves the entire body. I am a huge believer in the last one. I know some folk simply cannot do any physical activity, but most can do some – and the old Latin maxim *soluctor ambulando* (it is solved by

---

44 The best of these is *Anti-cancer: a new way of life* by David Servan-Schreiber. A lot of the figures in this section come from this source.

walking) can play a huge mental and physical part. If you can only walk five paces, walk them – and next week walk six. If you can jog or cycle a mile, do it – and next week add another hundred yards. If you are totally sedentary by choice, you are mentally dead and just waiting for the physical side of things to catch up.

There is also evidence that our immune system is sensitive to our emotional balance – weakening with stress and anger, and strengthening with serenity and support from family and friends.

Astonishingly, you could rewrite the above paragraph, almost word for word, and just substitute anti-inflammation for pro-immune system.

You could argue that cancer is now an epidemic (one in four people in the West will die of it) and it is now a disease of the rich – with our 'developed' (i.e. processed and refined) foods, 'developed' methods of farming and raising animals and 'developed' exposure to chemical products that didn't exist a century ago. The literature will give you hundreds of examples of what to eat less of (and vice-versa) if you want to strengthen your immune system and lessen inflammation – but I'm just going to home in on one to make the point. Sugar.

When, those millions of years ago, that animal dropped out of a tree and stood up in the East African rift valley, three things were noticeable: first, the similarity with Wayne Rooney was remarkable; second, he or she found the fingers and thumbs of one hand were opposable and third, as founder members of the hunter-gatherer club, they probably consumed about two kilos of honey a year. By the mid-nineteenth century, annual human sugar consumption had risen to five kilos. Today it is a staggering, monstrous, *seventy kilos* of the refined product. Along with white flour, via the release of insulin, glucose and another molecule you've never heard of, it is *the* friend of cell growth and inflammation. They are, effectively, fertilisers for cancer cells turning into tumours. Enjoy your cup of tea (with two sugars) and muffin (made with sugar and white flour).

These books about cancer come with endless advice on diet, and long lists of dos and don'ts. I simply remember the two basic issues that need addressing – immune system strengthening and inflammation reduction. Common sense, a bit of reading and some ability to recall will point you in the right direction more often than not. It is not always obvious, so here's a synthesised list of the good stuff, and I will bet that at least one surprises you:

- Green tea.

- Tumeric/curry.

- Ginger.

- Cabbages/sprouts/broccoli.

- Garlic/onions/leeks/shallots/chives.

- Carrots/yams/squash.

- Soy.

- Mushrooms.

- Tomatoes (cooked).

- Fish – preferably small, fatty fish.

- Probiotics.

- Berries.

- Citrus fruit.

- Red wine.

- Dark chocolate.

The surprise in there? Yup – cooked tomatoes, and that includes to-mato sauce. Ketchup is healthy. On receiving this news, I got my calcula-tor out. You can take a white bread roll (bad), cover it with butter (pretty bad), fill it with three slices of bacon (really bad) – and – hey presto – add seventeen squirts of ketchup and the whole thing is back to neutral. Sounds like a plan.[45]

I have not had an epiphany and I have not become a born-again health food freak. I repeat: you can take the boy out of Manchester but you can-not take Manchester out of the boy. Manchester is a place where they can put a meat and potato pie in a sandwich, and frankly, you would be ar-rested for openly selling some of the products on that list. If you are a male caught in possession of dark chocolate it is tantamount to a confession of homosexuality. But I'm not daft, and I am playing for big stakes now – and my diet (both the amounts and content of my food intake) has changed.

---

45 Do not try this at home.

I'm not making rules up here, or even relaying to you rules that others have put forward – for the simple reason that, in my experience, the Number One Rule of Cancer, and the pursuit of being cancer-free, is that there are no universal rules. Your cancer is strictly your own. The variables that go to make up your case – a combination of your genetic history, your state at the time and the location, aggression and extent of the disease – are literally infinite. If you are diagnosed with cancer, the plain and simple fact is that nobody – nobody – can predict the outcome. I am (at the time of writing) two and a half years into it, and am only just starting to figure out the routes on my Jencks Map. My surgeon and oncologist did the (make no mistake about it) heavy hitting, and I have come to terms with my mortality and my new normal. I've figured I have a couple of X-factors of my own that can help the pursuit, and there's a lot of not-quite-scientific wisdom out there you would be daft to ignore. All I've done here, as in the first two Books, is try to step outside my body and commentate on what's happened on stage – with me as one of the cast. As such, they are observations, and it is not a sermon, lecture or an instruction manual. I hope you have no cause to find it useful, and that its main purpose remains as that of Books One and Two – to give you a laugh at my missteps, and a few reasons to ponder about stuff.

I'm on the last lap of this section now, with just three more points to make.

First, if you are diagnosed with cancer, you will have a fight on your hands. If it is discovered early enough, you may never feel ill from the actual disease you have – but (trust me), you will feel ill from the cure(s). Before the end of it you will look different (i.e. worse) and your personality will change (worsen). It is easy to internalise this – it's your fight, isn't it? It's just you against some cells that can't stop multiplying isn't it? Well, no, it isn't just your fight. In all likelihood, you will have some family and friends who are close to you and, in some ways, they will have a harder time than you. You have an identifiable enemy and a physical fight on your hands. They have to stand by – helplessly, and frequently on the receiving end of your frustration – and watch somebody they love or care about suffer. Having cancer does not provide an excuse for treating them like dog shit on the soles of your shoes.

Second: when this kind of thing happens, something also happens to our basic communication skills. For some reason it becomes impossibly hard to tell someone close to you that you have cancer – but that's only a start of the problem. Your family and friends will then want to know what's happening to you. But they don't want to keep on asking, for the simple reason that they don't want to put you through the hoop of repeating the same gloomy speech again and again to different people. One of the great pieces of oratory of modern times was from (New York) Mayor Giuliani after the 9/11 bombings. While President Bush was nowhere to be seen, Giuliani fronted the TV cameras of the world and began his speech with the words 'This is what I know, and this is what I don't know'. I can't remember what came after, but what powerful words, and what a powerful idea in those circumstances – and there is a lesson there if you get hit with cancer. Technology helps here, with almost everybody having a mobile phone or email account today. Pick a squad of friends and family and just give them all the same message: this is what I know and this is what I don't know. It's not every day, or every week, it's just when a key stage is reached. Do that and there are no awkward conversations, no unnecessary repetitions and you don't have to try and remember the different things you told different people – and the people who care about you stop worrying about the unknown.

Third: from the day you are diagnosed with cancer, you will develop an unhealthy interest in statistics. There are thousands and thousands of them, and you will search desperately for one that means you can look to the future with more optimism. You'll become morbidly fascinated by median survival rates for breast cancer in females when you, in fact, are a male with a tumour in your bottom. When I was first diagnosed I ran a bath of statistics and just lay back and soaked in it. That all changed one day. I picked up on the results of a piece of research that indicated that the five-year survival rates for colon cancer (i.e. mine) for adult males (i.e. me) had *reached* fifty-three per cent. I chewed that piece of good news over for a bit. I was about two years into it, so (using all fingers) I calculated that I had a fifty-three per cent chance of living another three years. My non-linear mind then decided that what was ahead of me in three years was not a statistic, *it was a fucking coin toss.* From then on I have ignored all statistics, and that would be my advice to you. You will not beat cancer on the Duckworth-Lewis method.

My time is up, and I need a finishing sentence. I'm going for a bike ride to think of one, so you go and make yourself a cup of (unsugared) tea. I'll be back in a bit.

Well, here I am. That Rebel without a Clue, that Lord of the Files, has just done sixteen kilometres on his bike, and now he must go and change his Dyson.

Now, *there's* a sentence I never thought I'd write.

Epilogue

I genuinely thought I'd finished.

Some ten years after I wrote the first words of Book One, long before the cells in my body (the ones that became the root cause of Book Three) decided to cheerfully multiply, I thought I'd finished. Into my publishers went the manuscript.

My beloved 'publisher', sporting the profoundly unlikely name of Richard Burton, came back at me. He wanted something at the end, some sort of (in his words) conclusion, something to pull it all together.

I thought about this for quite a while, well into a second minute. My reply was a fine example of brevity: 'No'. What follows is a rough transcript of what happened next:

RB: 'I'm going to have another go. I think it needs it.'

Me: 'Needs what?'

RB: 'I dunno. You're the writer here. Maybe you could pull together some of the lessons others could learn from your experiences?'

Me: 'That's just arrogant bollocks. I have nothing to teach anybody. In the unlikely event that anybody wants to use something, they can write it down on the way through.'

RB: 'Er, well, maybe you could summarise some of your maxims, those that guided you through all this?'

Me: 'That's even more ludicrous. My only maxim is never have a maxim.'

RB: 'Christ, you do annoy me sometimes.'

Me: 'Good. Look, this is not a hill I wish to die on. How many words does this need to be?'

RB: 'It's not much – just something to end it all with. Maybe a couple of hundred words?'

Me: 'At the start of this sentence, this bit was running at two hundred and fifty-seven. Now go away, leave me alone and get publishing.'

RB: 'As I said, there are times when you annoy me. Intensely. What was the name of that gene you have again?'

Me: 'Which one? You mean the Wanker Gene?'

RB: 'That's the one.'